Teaching Matters:

How to Keep Your Passion and Thrive in Today's Classroom

SECOND EDITION

Todd Whitaker

Beth Whitaker

EYE ON EDUCATION
6 DEPOT WAY WEST, SUITE 106
LARCHMONT, NY 10538
(914) 833-0551
(914) 833-0761 fax
www.eyeoneducation.com

Library of Congress Cataloging-in-Publication Data

Whitaker, Todd, 1959–
Teaching matters : how to keep your passion and thrive in today's
    classroom / Todd Whitaker, Beth Whitaker. — Second edition.
    pages cm
    ISBN 978-1-59667-240-6
1. Teachers—Psychology.   2. Teachers—Job satisfaction.   3. Motivation
in education.   I. Whitaker, Beth, 1960–   II. Title.
    LB2840.W46 2013
    371.102—dc23

                                                                            2013000975

15 14 13 12 11 10 9 8 7 6 5 4 3 2 1

Sponsoring Editor: Robert Sickles
Production Editor: Lauren Davis
Designer and Compositor: Dan Kantor
Cover Designer: Dave Strauss, 3FoldDesign

Also by Todd Whitaker

Making Good Teaching Great:
Everyday Strategies for Teaching with Impact
Annette Breaux and Todd Whitaker

What Great Teachers Do *Differently*, Second Edition:
Seventeen Things That Matter Most
Todd Whitaker

What Great Principals Do *Differently*, Second Edition:
Eighteen Things That Matter Most
Todd Whitaker

Motivating and Inspiring Teachers, Second Edition:
The Educational Leader's Guide to Building Staff Morale
Todd Whitaker, Beth Whitaker, and Dale Lumpa

Feeling Great!
The Educator's Guide for Eating Better,
Exercising Smarter, and Feeling Your Best
Todd Whitaker and Jason Winkle

Dealing with Difficult Parents
(and with Parents in Difficult Situations)
Todd Whitaker and Douglas J. Fiore

Leading School Change:
Nine Strategies to Bring Everybody on Board
Todd Whitaker

50 Ways to Improve Student Behavior:
Simple Solutions to Complex Challenges
Annette Breaux and Todd Whitaker

Seven Simple Secrets:
What the BEST Teachers Know and Do
Annette Breaux and Todd Whitaker

Great Quotes for Great Educators
Todd Whitaker and Dale Lumpa

Also Available from Eye On Education

ABOUT THE AUTHORS

Drs. Todd and Beth Whitaker are both professors at Indiana State University in Terre Haute, Indiana. Todd is in educational leadership and Beth is in elementary education. Prior to coming to Indiana State, they were both teachers and principals in Missouri. Todd and Beth have three children, Katherine, Madeline, and Harrison. They have written more than 30 books and have presented to hundreds of thousands of educators around the world.

INTRODUCTION TO
THE SECOND EDITION

It seems like teachers are continually under fire. With new standards, increased scrutiny, complex evaluations, and the constant media crunch, at times we all probably ask ourselves, "Is it all worth it?" But then we see the look of understanding in a struggling student's eye, or we see a child who cannot wait to tell us something that he or she discovered independently, and it reminds us why we chose teaching—the most important of professions. At that moment, we smile and remind ourselves that it certainly is worth it.

This book is an attempt to help bridge the gap between the moments of anguish and the moments of joy. There are times we know we are making a difference, but our standardized test scores may not reflect the impact that we are having. At other times we may read an article in the paper about how teachers are overpaid and underworked. There are times we want to hurl the stack of term papers we are grading at 1:00 a.m. at the television when the latest attack on schools is being splashed across the screen.

Teaching is the most challenging, difficult, awe-inspiring, and rewarding profession that there is, and it is all of those things every day. There is nothing else like it. We chose education because we wanted to make a difference. And it does. Teaching makes a difference. It makes a difference every day. It reminds me of a Debbie Silver quote—*Teachers do what lawyers do, only for less pay, more judges, and a tougher jury.*

In this edition, we have added three new chapters in a section entitled Peers and Cheers. The first chapter is about how we can and must rely on colleagues in our schools for ideas and inspiration. The second is about social media and how it is available and essential to interaction and growth with others outside of the physical walls of our schools.

The third new chapter can help bring a little SPARKLE into your classroom and also into your heart. There are lots of things that separate the best teachers from the others, but one of them is how much praise and laughter take place in the classroom.

The best thing about being a teacher is that it matters. The hardest part about being a teacher is that it matters every day. Thanks for choosing to teach. Thanks for choosing to make a difference—now more than ever.

INTRODUCTION

Do you ever get the "how many more days until the holiday break blues?" Have you ever found yourself dreading Sunday evenings? Have you ever worked with someone who always seems to bring you down? Do you ever have trouble remembering why you chose education as your profession? Well, get ready to recharge your batteries. *Teaching Matters* will help you be at your best every day. Everyone who is in the education profession can benefit from this book. Teachers, principals, superintendents, and college professors—you all will learn how to:

♦ Rekindle the excitement of the first day of school all year long

♦ Understand how praise helps the giver as well as the receiver

♦ Approach every day in a "Thank God It's Monday" frame of mind

♦ Not let negative people ruin your day

♦ Be reminded of the importance of what you do

♦ Learn specific things you can do to have a great day at work

♦ Take charge of your frame of mind

♦ Fall in love with teaching, all over again

Let *Teaching Matters* help you bring back the excitement that made you an educator. Feel the pride you deserve in being in the most important profession that there is. This book is a way to thank yourself for being special. You deserve it!

TABLE OF CONTENTS

Part I

Why You're Worth It

1

The Value of Teaching

> **"** *Teaching is the profession that makes all other professions possible.* **"**
>
> —*Unknown*

If you are reading this book, then you have chosen the most important profession that there is—teaching. There is no other work we can do that is more valuable or essential. You are truly among the most influential people on earth. Yet, feeling like we are truly that critical is a great challenge. This book will help all educators to be revived, rejuvenated, and maybe even resuscitated. What we do is so important that we have to be able to remind ourselves of this every day.

Throughout this book, we will continually use the word "teacher." Understand this word "teacher" applies to everyone who is reading this book. It doesn't matter if you are a regular classroom teacher (whatever "regular" means), special education teacher, counselor, principal, college professor, media center specialist, cook, custodian, secretary, bus driver, or parent. If kids see us, then we are teachers. One way or another, we are teachers.

It is a funny thing, but whenever I hear teachers say they are having trouble getting motivated to go to work, one thought always occurs to me: "How do people who are not in education ever get motivated to go to work?" Though other people's jobs may be easier or less demanding, as teachers we have chosen a profession in which every day we have the chance to make a difference in the lives of many or even dozens of young people. If we can't derive motivation from the impact we have as educators, then how can others in less essential occupations EVER get fired up about their jobs? Yet it is a challenge that we all face.

Many schools, districts, and universities conduct teacher needs assessments, asking what their greatest needs are. In organization after organization, employees indicate their greatest need is greater morale. This is not inherently a criticism of anyone. Quite the opposite. What it really is is an understanding that high personal morale, or positive feelings, can never be too great. No matter how positive we feel, we wouldn't mind feeling even better if we could. Burt Reynolds used to say, "You can never be too rich or too thin." I don't know if he is correct in those cases, but I do feel that we can never feel too motivated or too inspired as educators. Knowing that we have a great chance each day to impact the lives of young ladies and gentlemen in our schools is a tremendous responsibility, but it is also a wonderful opportunity. Figuring out how best to take care of ourselves so that we can effectively achieve these results is the purpose of this book. As educators, we have to do it because there are numerous young people who are counting on us.

How Many of You Have Children?

One of my favorite questions to ask groups of educators is: "How many of you have children?" Typically if I am talking to large groups of teachers, four out of every five hands go up. Then I ask, "How many of you want your children to go to okay schools with pretty good teachers?" Usually only two or three hands out of the entire audience go up. I then say, "I guess those of you who raised your hands, your children must go to worse schools than okay and have poorer teachers than pretty good." The audience usually gets a good chuckle out of this. Then I ask the entire group this question: "How many of you want your children to go to great schools with outstanding teachers?" Every hand in the room goes up. I then say, "So do the parents of every student that enters the doors of our schools and classrooms each day. See, we have chosen the most important profession that there is and it is the one with the highest standards and the highest expectations of any other profession. The only acceptable standard is the standard of greatness."

Knowing that we have a great chance each day to impact the lives of young ladies and gentlemen in our schools is a tremendous responsibility, but it is also a wonderful opportunity.

That standard of greatness sounds intimidating, or even impossible, doesn't it? However, that really is the level of expectation we face. No wonder we are so tired at the end of each day! It really is a higher standard than other professions.

The other day I went into our local super discount store. It is probably the same chain you have been in many times. When it was time to check out, I happened to get in the line with the surly clerk. Have you ever been in that line? Probably way too often. Yet, while I was in the line with this less than giddy checkout person, I thought to myself, "I'll still come back here; their prices are pretty good." And anyway, the clerks are not necessarily too much better at any of the other stores!

Also, not too long ago, I happened to be in a long line at the bank. I was in too much of a hurry, and like every other educator I know, had way too many things on my plate. While in line, I thought to myself, "I don't even care if the teller rounds off!" After all, if we are in education then a few dollars either way doesn't even make any difference, does it?! All kidding aside, we easily tolerate less than perfect standards with almost every other profession we come in contact with. And the simple reason is, it is just not that important. However, when it comes to education, those standard increase dramatically.

The authors of this book are blessed to have three wonderful children, and we don't expect them to ever have one single teacher who "rounds off" in his or her interest. And we don't expect any of our children, any of your children, or any of the young people that walk through the doors of our schools each day to ever get one surly teacher. That is quite a challenge. It is a much higher standard than in other professions. Yet, we knew that was our challenge when we chose education. As a matter of fact, for most educators, that is precisely why they chose education. They wanted to make a difference in the lives of others on a daily basis. Every day we make a difference in the lives of the students we come in contact with. It is up to us to determine just how positive that difference is.

The Value of You

Yet, how can we be the teachers we need to be when we feel worn down to a nub? How can we be our best when we need a shot of enthusiasm or energy? The answer, of course, is we can't. That is why we have to take care of ourselves. If we do not take care of ourselves, then we cannot take care of anyone else either. This book will help all educators to revitalize themselves and even their careers by helping them realize that they have chosen the most important profession that there is.

We have to understand that every day our frame of mind is up to us. Each day we choose to view life in a positive light or a less than positive light. We determine if our cup is half full, half empty, or if it is just another dirty dish to wash. Each day we decide if school is about the 95 percent of the kids who put forth a pretty good effort every day or about the few students who are our biggest challenges. It is up to us to determine if the best part of our job is June, July, and August or Megan, Phillip, and Juan. No one else can do this for us.

Each day we decide if school is about the 95 percent of the kids who put forth a pretty good effort every day or about the few students who are our biggest challenges.

I truly do hope that each one of you has a supervisor, principal, or department chair who makes you feel worthy and valued each day. I also hope that each of you works in an environment where everyone is positive, productive, and professional. There is nothing that I would want more.

However, rather than just hoping, I insist that for all of our students it is up to us to make sure that the environments we create in our schools and classes truly are the best they can be. The field of education deserves our best, our students deserve our best, and most importantly, we deserve our best. Let's make sure that each day we wake up, look in the mirror, and remind ourselves that we have chosen the single most important profession that there is. It is the least we can do for ourselves.

2

Ten Days Out of Ten

"*A pro is someone who can do his or her best work . . . even when he or she doesn't feel like it.***"**

In baseball, getting a hit three out of ten times will get you into the hall of fame. In basketball, hitting half of your shots will get you into the starting lineup. In sales, having success even one out of four times might make you rich. But, in education, we have to treat our students with respect and dignity ten days out of ten.

Ten Days Out of Ten

One of my favorite sayings as a principal was: "You don't have to like the kids; you just have to act like you like the kids." It sounds funny, but it is true. Think of the best teacher in your school (besides yourself). I have great faith that that best teacher has students he or she likes less than others. However, with great teachers, even the students they like the least feel that they are the teacher's pet. It is because these great teachers treat every student with respect and dignity every day.

> If you act like you like the students, then it doesn't matter if you like them. If you don't act like you like the students, then it doesn't matter if you like them.

It is essential that every day we work to demonstrate how much we care for each student that we come in contact with. The clerk at that discount store we mentioned in Chapter 1 can have a bad day. Even the bank teller we mentioned can slack off a little, but if we have chosen education, it is critical that we come to work every day in a positive frame of mind.

If you ever question that it should be ten days out of ten, then ask yourself this. How many days out of ten would I like my students to be respectful and responsible? How many days out of ten would I like my students to come to class prepared and behave appropriately? How many days out of ten would I like my students to be cooperative and caring? If you answer these questions ten days out of ten, then the least we can do is to have the same level of expectation and effort out of ourselves. If we cannot do it as an adult, then it is completely unrealistic to expect the students we work with to even come close to this standard. And again, if we don't model this consistent, appropriate, and professional behavior, then the likelihood of those around us demonstrating it becomes greatly diminished.

In the book *Motivating & Inspiring Teachers (2nd Edition): The Educational Leader's Guide for Building Staff Morale*, I talk about my Uncle Larry. My Uncle Larry has this theory. His belief is that he doesn't want anyone running around smiling ruining his bad day. And believe me, Uncle Larry pretty much lives that. Do you work with anyone like that? Do you live with anyone like that? It is a real treat, isn't it? Well, in Chapter 15 we talk about how to keep yourself in a positive frame of mind even if you do work with or are around people who regularly have a sour

It is essential that every day we work to demonstrate how much we care for each student that we come in contact with.

disposition. However, I bring it up here because I first want us to make sure that we are not someone else's Uncle Larry!

Amazingly, even my Uncle Larry is positive some of the time. When it is time to eat or when he is in his recliner fully in control of the remote, he can even be pleasant (especially during his nap time!). However, it is the random snarls and put-downs that we most remember. If you work for a supervisor that is professional nine days out of ten, but humiliates you or someone else you work with once every two weeks, or even every two years, you spend much more time thinking about and talking about that one day than you do the other nine. You have to be aware that as a teacher you have to at least pretend to be in a positive frame of mind each day. And the first step to doing so is to realize that it is up to you. You don't have to be in a good mood each day; you just have to act like it.

Thank God It's Monday!

Dr. AI Burr, a retired educator who is one of my heroes, likes to say, "Great teachers come to work in a 'thank God it's Monday' frame of mind." When I share this with educators it always draws a chuckle. Sort of a "Yeah right—thank God it's Monday. Sure." However, the real question is, "Who determines our frame of mind?" And, we all know that the answer is, "We do." It isn't the school board, the parents, the dean, or the students—it is us. And, there isn't anyone else.

Dr. Burr shares a story that I'd like to paraphrase for you. A teacher was going home from work after a typically grueling day and stopped by the hospital to see his sister. He and his sister both knew she was never going to be leaving the hospital. When he arrived at her room she mustered up her usual smile and asked, "How was your day today?" The teacher moaned and muttered, "Oh, it was terrible. The kids were horrible, I had to deal with this awful parent, and the administrators were their usual incompetent selves."

His sister held up her hand as if to say stop and shared, "You may have enough days left to have a bad day, but I don't, so I do not want to hear it." What a valuable lesson for all of us.

It is an amazing thing, but I have yet to see one single teacher, young or older, who has enough days left to have a bad day. And I know for a fact that not one of the students that walk through the doors of our schools and classrooms ever deserves to have a bad day because of us.

The Best Teacher You Ever Had

I'd like you to take a minute and think about the best teacher that you have ever had. At any level—elementary, middle school, junior high, high school, or college—who was your best teacher? Think back and visualize the best teacher you have ever had.

Now, I'd like you to jot down adjectives or brief phrases that you would use to describe that person. Think of the characteristics of that teacher, and list them on a piece of paper. This is even better to do in a small group. If you have several people you can have each person share and describe the characteristics that each of your best teachers had. Amazingly, the best teachers that each of us has had share many of the same qualities.

On your list of characteristics or adjectives describing your best teacher, did you have any of the following? In my experiences with this activity, these are some of the most common responses:

- Caring
- Kind
- Challenging
- Sense of humor
- Energetic
- High expectations
- Knew you personally
- Fun
- Enthusiastic

Were any of these on your list? Examine your list and the one above. What kinds of things are on them? Most of the items are personal characteristics, aren't they? It is important to be aware that as adults, we choose what to be like. We make a choice each day how to behave and treat others. If you question this, ask yourself the following. "Could your favorite teachers have been unkind if they wanted? Could they act uncaring if they so desired? Could they have been lazy instead of energetic if the mood struck them?"

The answer is, of course they could have. They just chose not to or at least not to act like it. By the same token, we make that choice also. It is up to us to choose how we want to treat the students and others we come in contact with every day.

Every item on this list, and most likely, most of the items on your list, are all things that are "doable." We can choose to do them if we want to badly enough. Or we can choose not to. It is up to us. Though this is a lot of responsibility—to choose whether or not to be like the best teacher we have ever had—it is also a great opportunity. I am truly relieved every time I do this activity that "6 foot 5 inches tall with red hair and glasses" does not appear on the list. Because, if it did, then a lot of us would be unable to achieve that high level. Instead, thankfully, they are generally things that we can all choose to do if we want to. And we can choose to do them every day.

Interestingly, I have done this activity with a wide variety of groups and their lists look almost the same. It can be a group of teachers, principals, professors, parents, superintendents, or students and you cannot tell one list from the other. Also interesting are the words that have never appeared on the list. I have never seen the words "negative," "sarcastic," "bitter," or even "crotchety" appear on any list. These are all choices, too.

Be Your Own Reminder

I would also ask you to pose one more question to yourself. How many of us do you think have told that best teacher we just thought about that he or she was the best teacher we have ever had? Typically in a group of dedicated, caring educators, like yourself, approximately one-fourth have. I do not point this out in order to be critical. Instead I mention it as a reminder that even in a room full of professional teachers who have chosen to devote their lives to education, only about one out of four have told their best teacher what he or she meant to them. Thus, it is important for us to realize that at the end of a chapter or a unit, or at the conclusion of a semester or school year, not too many students are going to come up to us and exclaim, "You are the best teacher I ever had!" Yet it is important for us to remind ourselves that we may be many of the young people's best teachers and it is up to us to remember that, because there is a good chance that no one else will remind us. It also serves us to remember that we may have no knowledge of the type of long-range, positive impact we have on the young people we come in contact with. That impact goes far beyond anything that we may ever know.

And, before we move off the subject, if might be kind of neat, if it isn't too late, if you called, wrote, told, or even e-mailed that best teacher and expressed your admiration. I don't know about you, but I wouldn't mind hearing from a student I had five, ten, or even more years ago. Think how you would feel if your phone rang and a voice from the past on the other end said, "We were just doing an activity where we were to think about the best teacher we ever had. And . . . I thought of you."

3

We Are All Teachers

> **"** *If we don't model what we teach,* **"**
> *then we are teaching something else.*
>
> —*Unknown*

Any time young people come in contact with us, we are automatically teachers. Whether we treat others with respect and dignity or rudeness and derision, one way or the other, if someone sees us, then we are teachers. We may teach what is right and we may teach what is wrong, but there is no question about it, we are teaching. Understanding this is another reason that we must choose to approach every day in a positive light. If we do not show the young people that we work with that we are in control of how we feel, behave, and treat others, then many of them will not even know it is a possibility to live their lives that way. If we do not at least teach the children that, then we are missing out on teaching one of life's most valuable lessons.

So, It Is Possible to Enjoy Life!

As we grow as people, we learn that there are different ways to live than those that are most familiar to us. If we have students whose families normally interact with each other aggressively or violently, then the children coming from these families do not know that any other approach is possible.

I was reminded of something I experienced in college. I went to my girlfriend's house for dinner for the first time and could not believe what I was seeing and hearing. They actually talked to each other during supper! I never knew people actually did that. Oh sure, I'd seen it in movies, but I never realized that in "real life" families ever spoke to each other while they ate!

Whether this realization was good or bad, it then allowed me to choose how I was going to live my life. At that moment, I thought to myself how fun this family meal was, and I made a commitment that this was what mine would be like when I had children of my own. Now, every once in a while when my youngest is screaming about what the "Rugrats" did that day, I may not be positive I made the right decision, but it does reinforce how much our choices are within our control.

The students we work with may have never seen someone who could model for them how to treat others, how to use praise, and how reinforcing it is to show people respect and dignity. It is up to us to make sure that we demonstrate that for them each day. After all, like the saying goes, if we don't model what we teach, then we are teaching something else.

I have seen this same learning phenomenon occur in individual teachers' classrooms. I once worked in a school where the previous principal's approach to student discipline was to yell and humiliate. This person had been in the school for quite a long time and many of the staff members had adopted the same approach to discipline.

If we can demonstrate this love for lifetime learning for our students, then the likelihood of them approaching our classes and their future in this manner is much greater.

When I became principal of that school, I informed the teachers that I don't believe in ever yelling, using sarcasm, or arguing with a student. I remember one teacher named Betty who had readily adopted the former administrator's modus operandi and thought the best and only way to manage student behavior was to intimidate and punish. Together we had numerous conversations and I spent many hours in her classroom and with her in other teachers' classrooms who had a much more positive approach. Gradually she learned that you actually can manage students by using more positive and productive methods.

The real key to her change was the initial understanding that it is possible. Most of us do the best we know how, and it follows that one way to change is to know how better. If we can demonstrate this love for lifetime learning for our students, then the likelihood of them approaching our classes and their future in this manner is much greater. Making sure that we dream of future possibilities is often the first step toward getting there.

Teaching How You Take Care of Yourself

Demonstrating for students through modeling how we treat others is very important. Maybe the other thing that we can also show them is how we treat ourselves. This book has many ideas on how we can treat ourselves so that we can be motivated and inspired at work each day. However, it is also critical that we make sure students understand the things we are doing to help ourselves and that they understand why we are doing them. If we do this for ourselves it is helpful, but sharing it with our students may be as valuable to them as any "subject matter" we may teach.

Giving our students the gift of self-care and self-renewal is one that will keep on giving no matter what they choose to do. A few of our students will be fortunate enough to come from homes where these things are modeled and explained regularly. However, many others will not be so fortunate.

If we know someone who is a marathon runner, we often think of that person as lucky or a natural. I would bet, though, that the runner sees him or herself as dedicated and hardworking. Reinforcing for students the control that we have in the way we choose to treat others and, more importantly, choose to treat ourselves, is an essential part of being a teacher.

It is critical that we consistently work to teach others new things that they are unfamiliar with, not just reinforce bad habits that they may already have. It is similar to the concept of yelling at a student. Those students we are most tempted to yell at have been yelled at so much, it is ridiculous to think we can actually affect them with this inappropriate approach. Instead, we need to be able to teach these students new and appropriate methods that will serve them well in life.

The parallel to this is living our lives and treating ourselves in ways that will serve the students we work with most appropriately. It is essential that we as educators model for them and also explain to them why we do the positive things for ourselves that we do. Of course, one selfish benefit (and selfish can be good!) is that as we can use the students as an excuse to take care of ourselves. This can help us model for them, but equally as important, it can help us build the habits we need to be better professionals and people.

Teaching Our Peers

When we educators think about teaching others, typically we think about teaching our students. However, another critical role is teaching our peers. Though our instinct may be to think of teaching as in a traditional classroom setting, it may be more essential to teach them by modeling the way we handle ourselves.

Though we may know others who attempt to put us down or tease us in a mean-spirited way, the best way to alter their behavior is to model the proper way to interact. If we make it a point to compliment others, this can be contagious. I remember my very first year as a teacher, I was walking down the hall one day and the superintendent of schools was walking many yards ahead of me down the same hallway. He never looked back or saw me, but I still remember that he stopped, bent over, picked up a stray piece of paper off the floor, and threw it in a trash container nearby. That made such an impression on me that from that day forward I always made it a point, first as a teacher, and then as a principal, to pick up any paper thrown on the floor in the schools where I was employed. I'll even do this when I visit other schools. Interestingly, people all around me see this and begin to do the same thing. It doesn't matter who they are or what position they hold. It reminds me of the Dwight D. Eisenhower quote, "Leadership is the art of getting others to do things you want done, because they want to do them."

Here is another example you can practice on your own. If you find a busy door at a business or at the mall, watch how few people hold the door open for the strangers that follow them. Then, jump into the pack and hold the door for the next couple of people. It is amazing what politeness you will have started. This type of behavior is contagious.

If people attempt to be critical of you because you exercise, diet, or always seem to be in a positive frame of mind, it is only because they are not. If they had your determination and that of those who do work to take care of themselves, they would behave the same way you do. Understand, their only goal is to work to make others feel as bad about their own selves as they do.

Instead, realize that your doing the right thing is really the first step toward getting them to change. If people do not feel uncomfortable, they will never change. Having others around who are choosing to take care of themselves and live their lives in a positive manner is very disconcerting to people who are not. Make sure that you do not let them alter your drive to do what is best for you. As others begin to emulate your behavior—and they will—this will do nothing but increase the chances that even the most negative people will follow your lead. However, don't expect them to admit it, but they are very aware of how you treat others and how you take care of yourself. This is the first step for them as they begin to follow down the path you have carved. Good luck in your continuing journey!

4

It's Not Time—It's Energy

66 *If we don't have the time to do things right, when will we have the time to do things over?* **99**

—*John Wooden*

We all talk about not having enough time to take care of ourselves, or to do things we need to do. Chapter 9 discusses the value of using praise, but one of the biggest reasons given that we do not praise more is because we do not have the time to do it. Amazing, we can always squeeze in that one last gripe, whine, or complaint, but finding the time to do positive things for ourselves and for others often runs into roadblocks. Luckily, these roadblocks are most often set up by ourselves; thus, if we so choose, we also have the ability to remove them.

Effectively managing our time is very important. Educators live their lives with a full schedule every day. However, making sure that we find time for personal rejuvenation and inspiration is essential. We are well aware that we have to figure out ways to manage our time. Being able to increase the level of effort and energy that we have can often do more for us than saving a minute or two through time management. Raising our energy and excitement level is much more in our control than trying to stretch the day beyond the twenty-four-hour mark.

Increasing Your Energy

One of the biggest challenges we face is not so much a shortage of time as it is a lack of energy. It is startling how much we can accomplish when we are at our best. If we have a high level of enthusiasm and excitement, almost anything can be done. We work efficiently and effectively and are able to accomplish a myriad of tasks in a short period of time. By the same token, when we feel most tired or worn-out, even small obstacles or challenges can seem insurmountable. Being able to increase the amount of energy or vigor we have can do wonders for us. It can enable us to accomplish much more than we could with little energy and more time.

Think about how you feel the first days of school. You come to work with a spring in your step and a smile on your face. You have patience, tolerance, and seemingly unlimited enthusiasm toward what you do. Though there are still a limited number of hours in the day, you are able to fill them with your very best efforts.

Gradually, the days and school year tick along, and before we know it, we feel worn-out. Any task seems like a burden and even routine assignments seem unaccomplishable. Though we may more and more feel like there are not enough hours in the day, the real difference is the decreased amount of fuel we have in our personal tanks, which causes us to feel like there is a great shortage of time. But, the reality is that what we are really lacking is the energy that we need to accomplish our challenges. Instead of viewing things in a positive light, we begin to view them as an unfair or insurmountable burden.

Being able to increase the energy with which we face work and all of life's tasks is in our control.

Being able to increase the energy with which we face work and all of life's tasks is in our control. We just have to realize that and figure out a way to schedule taking care of ourselves into all of the things we face each day.

Recharging Your Batteries

Many people have found exercise to be an important source of energy for them. For years I got up at 5:15 in the morning and ran five miles. Though I am not particularly athletic, and by no means a runner, it is amazing what this did for my sense of self. And believe me, I am using the word "ran" in the loosest sense of the word. What I really did was allow myself to jog at whatever pace I was comfortable with and sort out my thoughts and be able to have some time just for myself.

There were many benefits, besides some potential physical health positives. I was always in a great frame of mind when I got done running. This allowed me to start the day in a productive mental state. It also was incredibly calming. If I just finished running five miles on a day when it was only 11 degrees outside, then I felt that for sure I could calmly and effectively deal with a challenging student or an angry parent that I might end up facing that morning.

Your initial thought may be that you are not a morning person. Trust me, I wasn't either. However, I chose that time because I felt that I was not taking away from my family. I would finish running at about the time that everyone else at home was getting up for the day. The difference was, I was now approaching the day with seemingly unlimited excitement and a positive frame of mind.

It may seem like I was "losing time" by spending forty-five minutes a day exercising. What I was really doing was now needing less sleep and "gaining energy" by being much more productive the rest of the day. It was really brought to light on days that I would not exercise. My patience, mood, and ability to accomplish were drastically reduced. Exercising did not take away my valuable time; it allowed all of my time to now be much more valuable.

Though everyone has different desires and abilities when it comes to exercise, even walking two "laps" around the school when we first arrive or at the start of our planning period can allow us to be much more productive and feel better about ourselves and our jobs. We can make taking care of ourselves a habit as easily as others make a habit out of complaining.

Scheduling Time to Rejuvenate

One other way that we can ensure that we take care of ourselves is to schedule it into our day. Think about the concept of praise. One of its most precious elements is that every time we praise, we feel better. Since we know this, it is important that we take advantage of this knowledge to help make ourselves feel better. If we can choose a day of the week, or a time of the day that we mark down in our calendars to write someone a positive note or to call a parent with good news, then we are marking down a time to make ourselves feel better also.

It is very much like how we feel when we devote some time or donate money to a charity. It may at first seem like we are giving something away, but in reality, we usually get as much or more in return. Being aware of this process and working to constantly rejuvenate ourselves is essential in being more positive and productive educators. Figuring out a way to make it work for us is something we all must do.

When I was a principal, I loved to visit classrooms. However, I learned that if I did not make leaving my office and going into classes a part of my schedule, I did not do it. In order to accomplish this, each Monday morning, I would find 10 to 20 minute slots each day and jot down parts of the school to visit. An example might be "Tuesday from 9:25 to 9:40, visit seventh-grade wing." Then I would make every attempt to get into the seventh-grade classrooms during this time. Though some principals say that they do not have the time to visit classes, I felt that I didn't have the energy to do my job if I didn't visit classes regularly. It helped remind me what education was about and allowed me to feel good about all of the positive things taking place in our classrooms.

Obviously many people reading this book are not principals, but the idea of marking in our calendars or lesson plan books activities that will help us to feel better about ourselves is for everyone. Some of those things may also benefit others, like praise, while others, like exercise, may seem more self-serving. However, keep in mind, that when we help ourselves to be more effective and productive we are also assisting ourselves in our efforts to be more valuable to others. Finding the time to help yourself can help you find the energy to help your students and those you work with.

Part II

Taking Care of Yourself

5

Viewing the Cup

> **"** *Whether you think you can* **"**
> *or think you can't, you're right.*
>
> —*Henry Ford*

The first time I heard the question "Is the cup half full or half empty?" was during my eighth-grade English class when I was thirteen. The teacher had presented the question as she was describing an excerpt from a novel we were reading. I remember looking around the room for the cup, as did many of my peers. When we finally realized there was no visual cup anywhere in that room, our immature, adolescent minds checked out of the moment. The words meant nothing to us.

It wasn't until later that quarter that I began to really understand the true meaning of these words. In the same English class, we were discussing the "horrible accident" in physical education that had occurred yesterday. The incident happened during a softball game. Patricia was batting and Jan was the catcher. During a warm-up swing, Patricia had no idea Jan was approaching her from behind to take her place behind the plate. During the follow-through on the swing, the bat struck Jan in the mouth. She lost her four permanent front teeth. Mrs. Fowler listened attentively as we shared the morbid details (everything got a bit bloodier with each telling). We also had learned, via our eighth-grade girls' telephone tree, that Jan would have fake front teeth the rest of her life! To us this seemed the end of the world.

When we had finally finished our gruesome tale, we all sat back awaiting Mrs. Fowler to be completely horrified and share in our dismay that Jan's life would never be the same. Instead, she began to ask us some questions. Was Jan still alive? Was her brain damaged in any way by the accident? Could she walk? Could she talk? Was she going to return to school in a few days? Would she be resuming her normal schedule? To all the questions, our answer was yes. "Well," said Mrs. Fowler, "is Jan's cup half full or half empty?"

Making the choice to see the positive in our workplace will always make the job easier and a more pleasing journey to embark upon each day.

Her simple questioning of an event that was real to us finally enabled a group of rural eighth graders to understand where the elusive cup was. The cup was in our own minds and our own perspectives. There was no doubt what had happened was terrible and we felt tremendously sorry for our friend. But the incident could have been much worse, and fortunately the damage was easily repairable. We learned about the importance of viewing events in our lives through a lens that allows us to see the cup as half full, not half empty. I still see Jan every year when I return home for visits. She probably has the prettiest smile of all the members of the former eighth-grade telephone tree.

In our everyday lives as teachers, we have literally thousands of opportunities to "view the cup." Making the choice to see the positive in our workplace will always make the job easier and a more pleasing journey to embark upon each day. It molds a mental framework that allows us to be energized by our positive perspective.

I am always reminded of an excellent example of "viewing the cup." When I was a principal, we often had visitors come to our school to meet our teachers, observe in classrooms, and discuss curricular innovations. Most visitors arrived with a group of teachers and their principal. On this particular visit the teachers were meeting with a few members of my staff, so the principal asked me to take her on a tour so we could discuss some administrative issues. As we strolled down the hall, a group of first graders came in from recess. They bounced down the hall in a slightly crooked single-file line. There was some soft chatter, giggling, and wind-blown hair, and there were many smiles. The teacher was walking at their side, grinning, and enjoying a quiet conversation with one of the students. My heart warmed as I observed their entrance. I was waiting to introduce the teacher to the visiting principal when the principal turned to me and said between pursed lips and narrowed eyes, "A little rowdy and obnoxious today, huh?" I was so taken aback I couldn't speak. The teacher approached, completely unaware of what had just been said. Her eyes sparkled as she proudly asked us, "Aren't they precious!!??" These two women had viewed the same moment in time. One had chosen to see the beauty of the moment; the other had tainted it with harsh judgments and negative perspectives.

Is the cup half full or half empty? You must realize that this choice is completely and solely up to you. No one has this auspicious power except you. Use it in a wise and healthy way. Looking for the good in life can at times be very easy. Those joyful moments in which everything seems to be going your way make viewing the cup quite simple. It's the times when things might seem less than advantageous that it will be the hardest to overcome the temptation to see only what is going wrong at that time. The following section will offer some tips on how to regain a positive perspective when the negative has become too overpowering.

A Positive State of Mind

Viewing the cup half full is much easier when we are in a positive state of mind. There are times in our professional and personal lives when many things seem to go wrong at once and a negative perspective becomes easy. Pulling out of this negativity is possible, but you must be the catalyst for change. There are ways to regain a positive attitude and approach to life. Here are some suggestions:

1. *Find Positive People.* You know who those people are. Find them and be around them if at all possible. These are the people that can make you feel better because of their words, actions, and attitudes. Their love of life is contagious and you need to catch their bug! Just as when we hear people complain we are tempted to join in, being around positive people can carry over to our frame of mind also.

2. *Laugh.* Find some outlet that will enable you to laugh and engage your sense of humor. Laughing and smiling are healing instruments. Watch your favorite sitcom, read the comics, tell your favorite joke, or find people who make you laugh. I have one coworker who can make me laugh until I cry. I seek her out in my low moments.

3. *Be with Your Friends.* These people know you and understand your inner workings. You can be honest with them and they can be honest with you. The comfort you experience by being with them can translate into a positive frame of mind.

4. *Find Time for Your Family.* Who best can make you realize how important life is and how blessed you are? Family gives us focus and provides that warm zone of well-being all of us need on a regular basis. When losing sight of what really matters, spend time with your loved ones. You will find yourself gravitating back to a productive outlook on life.

We close this chapter with a list of teachers' suggestions, "Taking Care of Ourselves" from Bobbi Fisher's *The Teacher Book: Finding Personal and Professional Balance* (2000, p. 96). These tips might help you to keep seeing the cup half full, not half empty.

- Write in my journal.
- Listen to music—classical, Cajun, jazz.
- Listen to music in my car—helps me to slow down.
- Stay with friends in an expensive motel and watch movies all night long.

- Shop.
- Get involved in a project.
- Bowl twice a week.
- Go to exercise class.
- Walk.
- Read friends' recommended novels during the summer.
- Take bubble baths and listen to relaxing music.
- Watch the sunset.
- Play Scrabble.
- Go to church.
- Pray.
- Go out with friends who are not teachers.
- Tell myself that I will only do schoolwork for a specific amount of time, and then stop.
- E-mail, Facebook, or tweet a friend.

6

Attaboy/Attagirl

"*People who feel special, act special.***"**

As educators, we spend a tremendous amount of time and energy taking care of others. This may include solving problems, listening when others are upset, or working to increase the morale of the students we work with. We wrote this book knowing that the ability to accomplish these tasks is an essential part of being an educator. However, this chapter is devoted to taking care of the most important person in your school—**you!**

Thinking Selfishly!

The idea of thinking selfishly may seem offensive to teachers. After all, we are in a giving profession. However, if thinking selfishly can assist us in the ability to be more effective in giving to others, shouldn't we consider it? It is critical that we focus on ourselves in order to be the positive and productive educators that we need and want to be. Let's look at how our frame of mind can affect many others.

If, as a teacher, I approach my students by starting off class in a negative tone, then the students will be in class with a negative attitude. Then, if when I ask them to get started on some independent assignment one of the students gives me a smart-aleck response, then my mood becomes even worse. This can be compounded no matter what professional position we have in a setting.

If, as principal, I am less than patient with a teacher, the teacher's frame of mind could easily be diminished. If that teacher then goes into the classroom and has a more negative approach to the students, then it is more likely that some incident will occur during that class that may result in an office referral. And, if I am the principal who handles discipline, then I will be the one who now deals with this problem. Thus, my disposition will be negatively affected. Again, if I do not have a way to make sure that my approach toward others is positive, then my interactions are likely to be even more negative with students and teachers, which, in turn, will create even more problems that I have to deal with.

These examples may be simplistic, but I have tremendous confidence that over time, this scenario is played out on a daily basis in schools. The opposite is also true. If someone compliments me, then I am more likely to pass along that compliment to someone else. If we can boost others' frame of mind, then they can do the same. It becomes self-perpetuating behavior.

It is like the old saying, "If a child feels stupid, he will act stupid, but if a child feels special, he will act special." It is like being on a diet. Compliment me on my appearance and I won't eat that last cookie!

If You Can't Take Care of You

Taking care of those around us and especially those we work with is a consistent challenge for any educator. However, in order to be able to sustain these efforts, which as teachers we must, it is important that those in these essential roles first take care of themselves. Because if we do not take care of ourselves, then we will be unable to take care of anyone else.

How can someone who is in the demanding role of a teacher, professor, principal, superintendent, department chair, team leader, etc., focus on himself or herself? When is there time? Is there any way to do it at work? Answering these questions is a critical link to having effective morale while at school. As educators we have to ensure that we have a positive outlook each day. And if we are not feeling very positive about ourselves, then it becomes difficult, if not impossible, to maintain this outlook. If we have a chip on our shoulder, then we do not want to be cheered

Whether they mean to or not, teachers establish the tone for the entire class.

up. Yet, it is essential for every teacher to maintain a persona that sets the tone for the classroom. Whether they mean to or not, teachers establish the tone for the entire class. When the teacher sneezes, the entire class catches a cold.

The educator has to be able to have outlets away from work that allow for this personal rejuvenation. These things can include exercise—one of the keys is to focus on how you feel when you are done, not how you feel while you are doing it! Our book *Feeling Great! The Educator's Guide for Eating Better, Exercising Smarter, and Feeling Your Best* can be of assistance in this area. Teachers can also attend professional conferences, spend time with family or friends, or even watch a certain movie or read a book that they know puts them in a positive frame of mind. One of my favorite things to do is watch the black-and-white holiday classic, *It's a Wonderful Life*. If, when I feel most down or sorry for myself, I can make myself sit down for two hours and watch *It's a Wonderful Life*, I am rejuvenated for weeks. But the real challenge is making myself do it when I least feel like it.

In addition to things they can do outside of the work day, it is critical that educators have things they can do while at work that allow them to reestablish a positive attitude and focus.

So, This Is Why We Have School

One of the challenges that all principals face is the number of problems that regularly come their way. They get to deal with kids when they are in trouble, parents when they are upset, and teachers when they have a problem. No matter how positive an outlook on life someone has, there is no question that this can be draining. When this occurs, principals have to be self-aware enough to realize what is happening and take the approach that they are going to do something to remind themselves why they became a principal.

This approach is essential for every educator. Everyone has challenges and a "most difficult" student or parent that one has to work with. We have to be able to consistently remind ourselves of the value of what we do. We have to continually refocus on what it is we do.

> *We have to be able to consistently remind ourselves of the value of what we do.*

I followed an approach that worked for me when I was a principal that I mentioned earlier. When I felt overwhelmed, I would go into some classrooms. Even if I could only do so for ten minutes, I made it a point to visit several teachers' classes. It reminded me of what school is all about. And, when I was the most down, I would go into my best teachers' classes. It is amazing, but even three minutes in your best teacher's classroom can provide a quick reminder of why you became an educator.

If I am feeling so sorry for myself that even visiting my best teacher's class does not work, there is one more room I could always visit. When I felt that life dealt me a rough hand, I would take five minutes and visit the multiple-handicapped classroom. I always felt that if I ever visited the multiple-handicapped classroom in my school and left feeling sorry for myself, then I was really in trouble. It is astonishing, but it never failed to help put things in perspective.

Though this may work for principals, many educators may not feel that they have the option of visiting classrooms when they need a boost. However, each of us can make this work. We all need strategies to use as preventive medicine. If you can set aside a few minutes each day to focus on the many positive aspects of your job, it can help you approach your work in a more positive light every day.

As a teacher or professor I could ask the three colleagues I respect the most if they would mind if every once in a while I could "drop in" on their classes. I would even tell them that I asked them because I admire them so much and they inspire me as well as their students. Maybe you could even just sit outside their classroom door or watch them at recess to see how much energy they give to their students. Then after your observation, drop them a note and tell them how much they affect you. What a boost for you both.

Obviously, one of the challenges in doing this is having time to do it. In using the example of visiting classrooms, other principals may have developed a system that allowed them to visit classes daily. However, for myself, I found that if I just hoped to get into classrooms that day I never did. Instead, I would pull out my personal calendar each Monday morning and write in times to visit classes each day. In other words, I would find 5 to 30 minutes on Monday, Tuesday, Wednesday, etc., to go into classes. I would also designate the grade level or part of the building I was going to visit. This allowed me to avoid going into the same few classrooms at the same time. So, on Monday I would visit the seventh-grade wing from 1:15 to 1:30. Tuesday, it would be the sixth-grade classes from 9:10 to 9:20, Wednesday, exploratory classes from . . . , etc. By scheduling this in my personal calendar, it forced me to set aside a few minutes for regular classroom visits. Keeping it private protected me during those inevitable times when something came up that I had to do so I could not go into classes that day. When I was fortunate enough to have an assistant principal, we would touch base on Monday morning and go through this process together. Thus, we would visit different classes, but we both made it a point to regularly observe instruction. This may be even more necessary for the mind-set of an assistant principal than for the principal! But it is an important part of taking care of yourself, so that you are more capable of taking care of others.

If you can set aside a few minutes each day to focus on the many positive aspects of your job, it can help you approach your work in a more positive light every day.

This same thing can apply to any educator. Though we are all very pressed for time, if we can write in our calendars or lesson plan books specific times to praise a peer, write a positive note to a student, or make a positive parent phone call, this time will result in a much more positive feeling about our jobs and ourselves. Recall that every time you praise, at least two people feel better and one of them is you. These same activities that can boost someone else's morale can also boost yours. It is amazing, but as educators if we have complimented a student or a teacher numerous times, that individual may actually be more likely to listen when we make a suggestion. Additionally, if we can continually acknowledge the efforts of others, their willingness to go the extra mile for us and more importantly, for their students, increases dramatically.

Praise for Students and Parents Can Be for You, Too

As a teacher, the more I contact parents and say positive things about their child, the easier my job becomes. My relationships with students and families get strengthened, their acceptance of future not-so-good news is enhanced, and their perception of me and my school is benefited. Again, maybe the most important aspect of approaching students and parents in this positive light is that it makes me feel better. Additionally, it is much easier to maintain a productive frame of mind if others treat me with greater respect, but regardless, every time we seek out these positive contacts we have a more appropriate and productive outlook on work and life.

Attaboy! (And Girl!)

In addition to all of the benefits we receive by recognizing the work of others, we still need an easy access support system of our own. If we are at home, maybe we can go out for a jog. But if we are in our office or classroom, we still need a quick fix. Something that every educator needs is an attaboy or attagirl file. We have to have a place where we keep positive notes we have received from our supervisors, peers, parents, or students. We can also include articles in the paper about our schools, inspirational sayings or quotes, or other mementos that remind us how important we are and how critical our roles as educators are. We may have a desk drawer where we put these things. We may literally have a file where we keep these reminders. It is essential that every teacher, principal, professor, and support staff member have a place to keep these gems.

We also need to be aware that as teachers and educational professionals, we probably have more opportunities to accumulate things in our attaboy and attagirl files than any other profession. For many people who are not in education, the only thing they can add is a paycheck stub. Yet, as educators we have many chances each year to acquire more in this special file.

When informally asking educators across the United States if they have a file like this, we found that about one-third of the teachers, professors, and principals accumulate these things for ready reference. The small number is a shame, because all professionals need such a source of rejuvenation. Each day we have student work that we might include. Teachers often receive notes, cards, etc., acknowledging their efforts. As educators we can be a great resource by providing notes of recognition and praise which others can save and cherish. The real challenge, though, is not developing an attaboy or attagirl file. The real challenge is when we least feel like it, when we most feel sorry for ourselves, when we are at the bottom of our self-worth reservoir, taking our file out and reading it. And, as teachers, we must do this.

Bob

I'd like to share an example from my attaboy file. Sharing it gives me a boost and maybe reading it can do the same for you. My first year as principal was in a small community in northwest Missouri—Hopkins, Missouri. That year I was principal and varsity boys' basketball coach in a school with about 225 students in grades 5–12. I was 25 years old when I got hired and was excited about having the chance to blend two careers by being both a junior-senior high school principal and a varsity basketball coach.

The varsity basketball season was about to start and tryouts were in just a few days, when a student named Bob came to my office after school and said he wanted to ask me a question. Bob was a senior that year and was in our mentally-handicapped classroom. As a matter of fact, he was pretty much self-contained by himself in that room and had been for many years. I was surprised that Bob wanted to chat, but I invited him into my office. I couldn't imagine what he would want, and really had no inkling of what brought him to my office that day.

Bob came in, sat down, and asked just one question. "Coach, could I be on the varsity boys' basketball team this year? I haven't ever played basketball before, but it is my senior year and I was really hoping that I could be on the varsity team with the guys." As you can imagine, I was quite taken aback. However, after only a moment's hesitation, I said to Bob, "Why sure, I'd love to have you!" We shook on it and Bob skipped out of my office.

That night I wondered what I was getting myself into, but I decided it would be good for Bob and good for the entire team. It might even be good for the school and community. And, it might, just might, even be good for me.

The next week when practice started, Bob was on the varsity boys' basketball team for his senior year. No only had Bob never played basketball before, he had some other somewhat limiting factors. Bob was 5 foot 6 inches tall. Bob had almost no basketball skills. He couldn't pass, he couldn't shoot, and he couldn't dribble. As a matter of fact, the only basketball thing he could really do was foul. And, he had that down to a science.

Well, the season started out and as you can imagine, Bob didn't really fit in with the team. Though he had been in school with the other guys for years, they did not really know him and he did not really know them. He spent most of his day in a self-contained classroom with few or no other students and certainly no other VARSITY basketball players. I was beginning to be concerned it would be a long, uncomfortable season for Bob.

We were nearing the Christmas holidays and one of the things that I always did as a coach was, in lieu of having varsity practice one day, I would load all of my boys onto a school bus. Then, I would personally drive that school bus around to all the retirement centers in the area and I would unload the varsity boys and we would go into each of the senior centers and sing Christmas carols for the residents.

You can only imagine what 16-, 17-, and 18-year-old boys thought about singing in public—especially the varsity basketball team! Each year, they would typically try to hide behind me and just mumble the words to the songs. However, this year was different. This year we had Bob, and Bob had no inhibitions about singing in public. He jumped right up to the front, and as loud as he could, Bob would warble each of the songs. As a result, this took all the pressure off the other boys and they happily joined Bob in song.

The result of all of this is that now Bob fit in. Because now, Bob had contributed. He was part of the team. Then something happened that changed my life and changed every player on that team's life. Each year at one of the practices over the holidays, I would pull out the goals that we had set at the start of the year. We then, as a team, would revisit these goals, to see if any of them needed to be changed. Sometimes we would add a goal, sometimes we would change a goal, and sometimes we would need to eliminate one of the goals we had set at the start of the season (for example, undefeated season!).

This year, at a late December practice, when I started to discuss the goals we had set at the start of the year in October, one of my varsity starters raised his hand. I ask him what he wanted and he said, "Coach, we were talking in the locker room when we were getting dressed before practice, and we, as a team, have decided that we want to add a goal to the list for the second half of the season." Curious as to what they could have possibly decided in the locker room, I asked the starting forward to continue. He said, "We would like to add the goal of getting Bob a basket in a varsity game." I almost cried right then and there. I could not have been prouder of a group of young men than I was at that moment. Somehow I got myself composed, and I said, "I will add it to the list." The player then added, "We'd like it to be our number one goal."

It may seem to you like this should have been an easy goal to accomplish. However, you have never had the opportunity to see Bob play basketball. Not only did his skill limitations make this a difficult challenge, but the consistency with which he fouled compounded this even more! Typically, when Bob got in a varsity game he would have no shots, several turnovers, and would foul out in just three or four minutes of playing time. Sadly, as the season went along Bob did not score. As a matter of fact, Bob did not even get a shot off in a game.

The other team always was very aware when Bob checked into the games. He looked very different than the other students. Additionally, Bob had a terrible time getting open to receive a pass. Bob was so slow and awkward that he seldom even touched the ball in a game. And, when he would, the opposing players would immediately steal it from him.

So the season was winding down, with little hope in sight to achieve our top goal of getting Bob a basket in a game. As a matter of fact, we only had one game left—our final home game. At the conclusion of practice the day before our last game, I called the players together and announced to them, "Guys, tomorrow is our last home game. I am going to start our five seniors." Every player on the team knew that one of those five seniors was Bob.

Bob was very excited. But what made me the proudest was that the entire team was excited. Even the player who was not starting this game because Bob had taken his place in the lineup was grinning from ear to ear.

The next day, when we finally got to tip-off time, a very nervous Bob was introduced with the starting lineup. You could hear the murmuring from the crowd as Bob's name was called. I could only imagine what the other team was thinking when Bob ran out to greet the other starters. Though Bob getting the starting nod may have filled our team with excitement, it did not seem to cause much of a change in Bob's abilities.

After about the first three minutes of the game, Bob had made several turnovers, had not taken a shot, and had committed three fouls. I had no choice but to take Bob out. We still had a chance to win the game and that was important to the entire team. So, when I took Bob out of the game I put my regular starting five back in. And, maybe it was because of the emotion of senior night, maybe it was the boost that starting Bob had given, or maybe it was fate, we ended up getting a really big lead that game. That was not too common that year as we ended the season with 11 wins and 12 losses. Importantly though, the big lead gave me a chance to put some substitutes into the game. The substitutes, of course, were led by Bob.

We continuously worked to get Bob the ball, but just as regularly, the other team kept stealing it. Bob's lack of foot speed kept him from ever getting open enough to get the ball, much less to actually get off a shot. Almost immediately when Bob checked into the game, the opponents quickly discovered that we were working to get him a shot, and they regularly and easily prevented that from working. Even the poorest player on all of our opposing teams could guard Bob and keep him from scoring.

I knew this was our last chance and Bob's last chance at scoring, so I called a time-out. We had to figure out something that would get Bob open so he could have a chance to score. When the team huddled over on the sideline, we came up with a plan. I told them, "You four players (the others in the game besides Bob) are going to be down at this end of the court playing defense and rebounding. And Bob, you are going to stand at the far end of the court underneath our basket and wait for them to throw you the ball."

When we broke the huddle, it was one of the strangest sights I have ever seen. Five players on the other team were attempting to score on four players for our team while Bob was at the far end of the court underneath our basket. And, to top it all off, Bob had his hand in the air! It looked like he was trying to ask the referee a question.

I realized though that Bob had his hand up because one of the things we always talked about was whenever he got open to put his hand up. Poor Bob, he was down there so long by himself that his arm had to be exhausted.

Finally, the other four players would get the rebound and they would turn around and whip the ball down the court to Bob. This sounds like a great solution. The only problem was that they couldn't really throw very well, and Bob was even worse at receiving a pass. I quickly realized that in order for Bob to catch the pass it was going to have to be a perfect throw. So, once again, I called a time-out.

I told four of my starters to check back into the game. We had to have players that could throw a catchable pass so that Bob would have a chance of snagging it when it came his way. We broke the huddle and nine players headed to one end and Bob trotted down to the other. By now his arm was so tired from being open he couldn't even raise it above his waist.

My four starters were at the far end of the court and doing the best they could to guard the opposing five. Finally, they would get the ball and take off dribbling up the court. At that moment, one of the most amazing things I had even seen in a high school gymnasium occurred. The other team stopped crossing at half-court! Literally, nine players would stop at the mid-court line and a teammate would gently throw the ball to Bob. Well, Bob was now about to catch the carefully thrown toss. He would take a shot and miss, get the rebound, take another shot . . . and miss. Then, finally the ball would hit his foot and go out of bounds. As you can imagine by now, the crowd was going crazy rooting for Bob to score!

The other team would get the ball and we would start it all again. The opposing five would come down, attempt to score, and finally we would get the ball. The team would take off dribbling, nine players would line up at the half-court stripe, and Bob would be tossed the basketball. He would shoot on one side and miss, scurry after the rebound, shoot again, and the ball would fly over the rim out of bounds.

The game was winding down to the final seconds, the crowd was almost frantic, and finally, at the buzzer, Bob scored! I am sure that the timekeeper even held the clock! The reaction was as if we had won the state championship, only so much sweeter. It was a surreal scene on the court and in the stands! I felt like my own son had hit the winning shot.

The joy on the team was wonderful, and we had quite a school-wide celebration. And, to top it all off, the editor of the *Hopkins Journal*, a local newspaper, ran a column the next week:

I know that this is going to come as a surprise to you, but underneath this rugged John Wayne's shell, is the body of a marshmallow. The meaning of all of this is, I can remember my big hit in little league, my great catch, my great basketball game where I scored 10 points, my three high school wrestling wins, one a year, for three years, including the win over the boy I told the match was over, he rolled off and I jumped on him, and the time I accidentally kneed a kid in a tender spot. These aren't even as great as they seem to be, as they were all in intermural competition. There aren't any letters on my jacket, in fact, I don't even have a jacket. In high school I went out for baseball, only to hear when I got on the field, "It's time for me to make my first cut, Lohman, take a shower." I went out for basketball in college, to hear, "This is the last uniform, you might as well take it." I was 6'1" at the time, and weighed 139 pounds, the uniform was made for Kareem, and I ran onto the floor with the pants held up with safety pins. I have never had a good relationship with coaches, and even to this day, have a hard time talking to almost all of them. Kind of a "We're in a different universe" attitude.

Not to put anyone down, cause I think our coaching staff has improved a lot this year, but I think we got a real jewel in Coach Whitaker. As he told me, he believes sports should be a growing experience, if you don't know what he means by that, you weren't at the game Friday night. If you were at the game, you know what he means. The man deserves a lot of credit, let's leave it at that.

—adapted from the *Hopkins Journal*

We are all blessed to have known, impacted, and influenced our own Bobs; however, the challenge for me, just like the challenge for every educator, is not accumulating things like this in my attaboy file. The challenge for me, just like the challenge we all face, is when I least feel like it, when I most feel sorry for myself, taking this column and the cards and letters I received from Bob out of my attaboy file, and reading them. Returning to the moment of our most touching experiences can help us "emotionally revive" when we most need to.

We cannot afford to approach our work, and more importantly, to have contact with students, without a positive outlook. It is critical that all educators approach each day in a positive frame of mind. We have to take care of ourselves because we have chosen a profession where each day we are taking care of so many others. You are worth it.

7

Could I Have a Refill Please?
Opportunities for Renewal

"*Change is inevitable; growth is optional.***"**
—Unknown

When I began teaching many years ago, the venues for professional growth were very limited. Workshops were regional, the state conventions were too expensive, and no one had ever dreamed of bringing a national speaker to our small school district. It seems now that the possibilities are endless and there are financial support programs to allow teachers quality professional development. As a teacher, you must become proactive in your quest for professional renewal. Look for conventions, assist in coordinating workshops for your school, and create learning opportunities that meet your needs. This chapter will touch upon some paths you can take toward renewal of your teaching commitment.

Workshops and Conventions

You might be thinking that you don't need to attend another workshop or hear another speaker at a convention. If you are nodding your head in agreement, please think again. We all must continue to listen and learn throughout our careers. No matter if you are just beginning your teaching career or drawing it to a close soon, the need for rejuvenation is always present.

Maybe you think you have learned all there is to learn or heard the speaker before. Let me ask you this. Why do we read books more than once? Why do we choose to see certain movies again and again? It is not only because we enjoy them, but also because we learn something new or see something different each time we allow ourselves to indulge again. It is the same with good speakers and quality workshops. You always think you will remember everything that was said or demonstrated, but we all know the reality. You return to the classroom, try a few things, and lose track of the rest of the content presented. Hearing and seeing something again can remind you of what you learned and provide the opportunity to refresh your memory of the ideas that slipped away on your trip home.

Earlier we mentioned the Christmas classic *It's a Wonderful Life* starring Jimmy Stewart. My husband and I watch this movie every year (sometimes more than once). We know most of it by heart and can dialogue back and forth with each other certain key scenes in the movie. Why would we choose to spend well over two hours watching a movie that we can recite from memory? It is all about the way we feel when the final credit rolls past us. It is all about the tears we annually shed during the final five minutes of the movie. It is all about remembering exactly what is important in life. When that movie is over, we approach life with more reverence and view our family and friends with renewed love and respect.

This feeling I speak of can come from listening to a dynamic speaker (perhaps more than once). It can also come from attending a great workshop (perhaps more than once). These feelings enable you to return to your teaching with restored enthusiasm. Actively seek information on state and national conventions and workshops. Don't let price or location deter you. Often school districts have professional development budgets to support you, or state departments have grant opportunities that will help pay for your learning experience.

These professional gatherings are not only great opportunities to learn from experts, but also present a time for networking with your colleagues away from your own school district. Recently I heard a teacher discussing the fact that her school district was choosing to bring well-known experts to her school versus sending teachers to workshops. She was excited about the opportunities that were being presented to her, but mentioned that she missed meeting teachers from other schools across the state. She had enjoyed being able to share ideas and gather different perspectives. I think her point is well taken. School districts should find a happy medium that allows for some expert "in-house" staff development, but they must also provide opportunities for educators to get away from their known environments and communicate with other professionals.

Retreats

A retreat is a time to leave behind the routines of school and home. It is uninterrupted time to focus on professional growth and personal rejuvenation. Retreats can vary in length of time and can be close to home or far away. They can be coordinated by your school or by another organization to which you belong. The most important aspect of the retreat is the physical time away from school. A retreat, in the purest sense of the word, should be a time for quiet, rest, and reflection. This reflection has the potential to refuel your engines and help your work take on deeper purpose. You are given time to not be "clock conscious" or "bell driven." The focus and renewal that can occur during a retreat can work to solidify your professional beliefs and goals.

Group Retreats

Most schools have regular in-service staff development for teachers. These are often half-day workshops, usually in the afternoon when the children have been dismissed at noon. Sometimes they are a full day before school starts, a Saturday during the school year, or a day at the end of the school year. They are even week-long events held during summer months. These full days and weeks are often called retreats because of the length of time involved.

Often schools will have a committee of teachers that plans and organizes these staff retreats. Empowering staff members to take on traditional administrative roles is becoming very common in shared leadership plans in schools. If you find yourself on one of these committees, the ideas presented in the following section can help guide your development and implementation of successful staff in-services or retreats. Modify them to suit your needs and elaborate to add interest to your occasion.

Settings That Inspire

Often in-services are held in the school itself to keep staff from having to travel if they are already at school. If you choose to stay in the building, give thought to where you will house your meeting. Make sure the chairs are comfortable and there is plenty of table room for participants to take notes and peruse handouts. The lighting should be appropriate and avoid crowded spaces if at all possible.

If a full-day retreat is planned, think about trying a location away from school. Removing staff from the all-too-familiar school setting can be enjoyable and motivational to them. They aren't tempted on break to run to the classroom and pick up something or check voice mail or e-mail. There is no intercom disrupting the meeting or bells ringing to remind them of school functions. When considering alternate locations, be open-minded and creative. Think about your community and some of its important structures. Some locations can include art museums, historic buildings, conference rooms of local corporations, and meeting rooms at country clubs, hotels, or restaurants. If you live in a town that has a college or university, these settings usually offer a variety of options for quality retreat experiences. In addition, local and national parks supply multiple options for giving the staff a unique experience. Besides the obvious variety of meeting locations, many parks have team-building and leadership-training courses. These provide the faculty an opportunity to complete a physical activity course that builds group support and team cohesiveness.

Inventive Invitations

If this is an event you want people to consider as special and important, send them invitations. The invitation might be a simple piece of colored paper with information about the event on it. Include graphics or clip art when possible. Think of creative wording to entice them to come to the workshop. A humorous or inspirational quote can catch attention also. Look through books, the Internet, magazines, or even greeting cards to get ideas. If the retreat or event is extremely important or special, consider having invitations printed. Most computers have endless capabilities to print stylish and artistic products on eye-catching paper or correspondence cards. Attaching something to the invitation can also ensure that it will get noticed. A crayon pasted to the announcement of an art workshop or a ribbon in school colors attached to a staff in-service notice can catch the readers' attention and give them a sense of the meeting. An invitation also gives the participant something concrete to refer to and keep posted as a reminder. Be creative and imaginative when inviting people to your next gathering.

Be creative and imaginative when inviting people to your next gathering.

Thoughtful Arrangements

Take the time to survey the room and furniture available for your event. Are there ways to rearrange the existing format to better suit the needs of your workshop? Do you want people in small groups? Can tables be angled to better view the speaker's location? Are the chairs comfortable for adults to sit in for a period of time? Creating a comfortable and functional room arrangement will be appreciated by participants and create the optimal learning environment for them.

Make sure participants have access to clean and adequate restrooms. Be ready to supply directions as to their location and have someone check them periodically to make sure they are continuously well-maintained.

Identity Crisis!

Consider supplying name tags for your event if participants don't know each other. According to Feigelson (1998), name tags serve three major purposes:

1. They allow people to address each other by name.
2. They provide additional information about the person that can stimulate conversation and help people make connections.
3. They help elicit a smile and create an inviting, friendly, positive tone. (pp. 32–33)

The author also suggests some creative ways to add information to a name tag that will promote conversation and enjoyment. People are instructed to write their name on their tag and some additional items. The following are her ideas:

♦ *Add the name of someone who makes you laugh.* This can be a writer, movie star, comedian, or someone you know.

♦ *Three numbers that are all significant to you, for any reason at all.* She relates that one administrator put the numbers 3, 1, and 10 on her name badge. Three was the number of grown children she had; one was the number of husbands she had; and ten was the number of years it had been since she last cleaned her kitchen "junk" drawer.

♦ *A significant personal or professional first you've had in the past year.* This reflective approach gives participants current information about their peers.

♦ *Three things about me, two of which are true.* This can promote a guessing game regarding which of the three things isn't true. It can also foster the discovery of common interests.

♦ *Headlines.* This can be anything that the person feels is important in his or her life. It could relate to something personal or professional. Some examples might be:

"Goal Achieved!" "New Grandparent!" "Top of Desk Finally Seen!" "Guess Who Got Married!"

♦ *Something positive about me that people in the room probably can't tell just by looking.* Again, these ideas can be about anything. It is an opportunity to spread good news, share a personal accomplishment, or relate some obscure piece of information about oneself. Quality conversation and common interests will evolve from this activity.

♦ *Something I could use help with.* This can generate conversation and potentially solve problems. Requests for help can emerge from your home life or professional life. From "Running Toilet" to "Job Leads," this name tag addition ensures lively conversation.

♦ *Something I know quite a bit about.* This gives participants the chance to share their strengths and potentially find resources for future use. Examples include "website design," "antique hunting," "playing the piano," "home renovation," or "marathon training."

Creature Comforts

Creature comforts refer to the things you can do and items you can provide to make participants more comfortable throughout their experience. This is a critical element for any renewal event, but very important for retreats or workshops that last more than a couple of hours.

Greeting people as they enter the workshop is always a positive and professional way to set a pleasant tone for the workshop. This activity requires no money, just your friendly smile and words of welcome. This is especially important for activities where some participants don't know anyone. You can become an immediate connection for them and help them begin to feel comfortable in this new environment. Having background music playing and a welcome greeting on the overhead screen can also add to creating comfort from the start.

Food and snacks are always important features to be provided by workshop planners. Providing coffee, juice, muffins, and fruit is always a good way to begin a morning workshop. Such snacks give people a chance to nourish themselves, interact while eating, and have their familiar cup of morning coffee. Beginning in this fashion helps people settle in for the day and start to feel comfortable. A midmorning snack of fruit and drink can usually help people continue through lunch. If you are providing lunch, make sure you have had detailed conversation with the caterer about numbers needed and the lunch entree. It is important to always have enough food and ensure that a variety of options are available. Keep in mind that some people are vegetarians or may have allergies related to certain foods. A varied selection of items helps these people make appropriate choices. Afternoon snacks are a must! This can often be the hardest time to keep your audience involved and happy. Popcorn, pretzels, Cracker Jacks, fruit, and (of course) something chocolate can keep people nourished and energized. Offer soft drinks, water, and perhaps even coffee or hot chocolate (especially during cold winter months). Also consider keeping a basket or dish of mints, hard candy, and chocolate kisses on each table at all times. This gives participants an edible option when it's not time for a scheduled snack or lunch break.

Be cognizant of room temperature and lighting. Make sure the room is not too hot or too cold. Provide adequate lighting for note taking and reading of materials. These may seem simple and fundamental, but we have all seen the mood of an event deteriorate quickly due to lack of attention to these elements.

Supply participants with an agenda, handouts, notepads, and pens or pencils. In their hurry to get to a workshop, many people forget these items and are relieved when they are provided. It lowers their level of stress and connects them immediately with workshop content. Often, local businesses or corporations will donate paper and pens for your event.

Door prizes also add an element of fun and excitement to your workshop. These prizes can be items donated or purchased through your budget. Following are some suggestions for educational retreat door prizes: a supply of markers, pens, and pencils; brightly colored packs of Post-it notes; a selection of colored paper; computer software; books; dinners at local restaurants; gift certificates to a teacher store or book store; weekend packages at a local resort; staff T-shirts, mouse pads, or coffee mugs; or a morning at a local spa. The options for door prizes are only limited by your creativity. Many hotels, restaurants, and stores will donate items when they know they will support the local schools.

If possible, have centerpieces for the tables that promote the theme or purpose of your meeting. One high school had a spring retreat and provided potted plants on each table. They were given away as door prizes at the end. During a January retreat, another school had its art students create centerpieces with a snowflake theme. These were especially appreciated as they were a continuous visual reminder of why they were there . . . in the best interest of students.

Hey, Give Me a Break!

Schedule breaks into the workshop or retreat. People need the opportunity to move around, interact, and refresh themselves. Always allow at least ten to fifteen minutes for a break. Any shorter time than this can make participants rush and return feeling like they didn't even have a break. Use this opportunity to play music and have an inspirational quote or humorous cartoon on the overhead screen. When announcing the break, give them a sneak preview of the exciting event that will follow the break. Perhaps there will be a door prize drawing or tell them a surprise will await them when they return. The surprise can be a fun activity, a trinket placed at each seat, or a humorous story or joke.

Also consider getting feedback during the break. Set out Post-it notes with markers and encourage participants to write questions, one thing they have learned, or comments on these Post-its during their break. The group then posts these on chart paper, a chalkboard, or even available wall space. It provides you with feedback and a sense of what needs the audience might have. You can address their questions during the remainder of the workshop.

Facilitate an activity upon the return from a break. This can help people refocus on the content and presentation. It might be a door prize drawing coupled with a reflective writing time to help the audience synthesize what they have learned so far. A human development activity (HDA) is always a good alternative. HDAs are activities that pull the audience back into the content in covert and overt ways. Some examples include: group listing of the "Top Ten Things We Have Learned," walking around the room sharing two things you have learned with other workshop members, or a group summary of workshop content on chart paper.

Keep Them Active

We are all aware that making human beings sit for long periods of time is not an optimal learning situation. When planning your workshop or retreat, create opportunities for movement and participant involvement. These can range from quick energizer activities to group project assignments during the day. There are many books that provide energizer ideas, and take the time to think about what you have seen done by outstanding presenters. Their practices can provide many good ideas that you can borrow and use at your next in-service.

Theme It!

If you plan a three- to five-day professional growth experience for faculty, consider giving it a theme. This theme can then provide inspiration for activities, setting, and creature comforts. I had the good fortune to work for a week with a school corporation on K–12 curriculum design. The committee that organized the event chose a garden theme and did an excellent job pulling this into the task of curricular change. The invitations were colorful and had clip-art flowers placed on the document. They transformed a nondescript high school study hall into a comfortable room that "spoke" the theme. They had inspirational growth and garden quotes on the walls, plants and fountains were placed throughout the room, a garden trellis invited everyone into the area where snacks and professional resources were available, the tables had garden centerpieces on them, the door prizes were donated by a local nursery, and each day began with an activity centering around growing and nurturing the curricular changes they were creating. The participants anticipated each day because they knew something creative and fun would be awaiting them upon their arrival. Much was accomplished during the week, and I attribute a great portion of the success to the wonderful job the committee did tying everything to the chosen theme.

Always Leave Them Feeling Good and Wanting More

It is important to have some thoughtful way of concluding your workshop or retreat. It can be as simple as a positive summary statement by you, the organizer, or as elaborate as a celebratory meal with presentations. Drawing closure to your event in an upbeat, motivating way leaves people feeling good about themselves and the workshop. It helps them synthesize what they have accomplished and learned. This enables them to see the value in the time they invested. Provide an opportunity for them to give thought to how they will use and apply the information to their classroom practices.

At the end of the week-long curriculum workshop I mentioned earlier, the organizers planned a tasty catered luncheon for everyone. At the conclusion of the meal, a school board member presented everyone with a certificate of participation beneath the garden trellis. This certificate was printed on botanical stationery, and they also received a laminated bookmark covered with pressed flowers—all inexpensive ideas, but very meaningful to the teachers who received them. The school board member making the presentation also gave value and importance to the job they had done throughout the week.

Drawing closure to your event in an upbeat, motivating way leaves people feeling good about themselves and the workshop.

Another easy treat to provide your group is dismissing them a few minutes early. People resent being kept longer than the designated ending time. Many have scheduled other events and delaying their departure creates feelings of negativity. Letting them go even ten minutes early is always a morale booster and helps them leave feeling there is time to spare in getting to their next meeting or scheduled appointment. They leave the workshop feeling upbeat and better in control of their time.

Giving people a small token at the end as a remembrance can also create good feelings about the workshop or retreat. These can be as elaborate or simple as your budget allows. For important, lengthy events, you might consider a specially designed T-shirt or plaque to commemorate the occasion. But for a half-day or day-long workshop, simply standing at the door and thanking everyone for coming will suffice. A special pencil or pen, a new mug, or a book that complements the workshop content are additional ideas for tokens of appreciation. Your planning committee might also consider a follow-up thank-you note to teachers for their participation. This personal touch can mean a great deal.

A Personal Retreat

We often think of retreats as small- or whole-group activities. These events are usually quite fun and invigorating, but I want to plant a new seed of thought for you. What about a retreat spent by yourself? A time just for you to take a quiet, uninterrupted look inward and work to calm and sort through the waves of your daily life. Ideally, we would love to think this would be done during a week-long respite at a spa in Arizona, but we all know that reality and finances probably negate this wonderful concept. As an alternative, what about just a few hours for yourself at least once a month? This will be your personal time of renewal and reflection. I would suggest that you try to make this an outing. Get away from your home and workplace. Even though you might be able to get the house to yourself for a few hours, the environment is still your home. Cleaning, laundry, phone calls, dishes, or paying bills will always be looming in your subconscious. You must physically get away from these surroundings to be able to really focus on yourself. The spot you choose could be a local library, park, or museum. You could even rent a room for one day at a local bed-and-breakfast or inn. Think about places in your community and neighboring towns that might present a quiet and secluded place for you to hibernate for an afternoon. Pack a small bag full of some favorite snacks and drinks. Take a professional book you have always wanted to read and a journal for thoughts and notes. Write down your professional priorities and goals. See if they are working together. If they aren't, use this time to think of ways the two can merge logically during your work day. Begin to write some personal reflection about your job and force yourself each time to end your writing on a positive note. Remember that the cup is half full, not half empty. You might find that the writing is so rewarding for you that you want to create something for a professional journal or newsletter. These venues need the voice of practicing teachers. Your rich experiences and perspectives enlighten all who read them.

Think seriously about indulging in a personal retreat. Life and job demands often do not allow us to take care of ourselves. You need something like this. We promise you will find it a pleasure and it will enable you to reconnect with why you became a teacher.

Study Groups

I remember the day that I watched Oprah launch her Book Club. I knew it would be a success because I had used this concept in my classroom with students. One must also note the unbelievable popularity of Oprah's Book Club as its enthusiasm spread across the nation. Adults were responding exactly the way students do. They love reading for pleasure, sharing their connections with the text, and listening/responding to others' thoughts about the book.

Teachers can use this same concept as they read and interpret articles and books. This concept links pleasure and practicality. Teachers read professional development articles/books of their choice. They then have the opportunity to reflect with their peers on the text and learn from this powerful process. Participants are asked to have read the article or a certain number of chapters in the book by the time the group meets. When the study group gathers together, they spend time reflecting, questioning, sharing, analyzing, and synthesizing the content of the book or article. These study groups can meet before or after school, at the school building, or at a site away from the school. They provide an opportunity for professional thought and sharing. In education, we don't often take the time to reflect upon what we read. We encourage our students to do this, but we don't practice it ourselves. Literature study groups allow teachers to discuss professional literature and learn from others' perceptions and analyses.

Another twist to this would be to have teacher book clubs or study groups that don't necessarily read only professional literature. These clubs could read historical and contemporary fiction and have meetings about these more mainstream books. One school district did this and found that teachers began to reflect upon their teaching (Goldberg & Pesko, 2000). Adjustments to classroom instruction soon emerged because of their personal experiences in the book clubs. These teachers began to abandon student activity and comprehension sheets, give students more choices, reduce requirements for journal writing, steer away from prescribed questions and answers, and teach students to say more about less. Based upon what they experienced in their own book club, they worked to make their classroom instruction meaningful, motivating, and relevant to the students.

Reflection

In our busy, whirlwind society, reflection is quite often a retooling agent that is not used. Who has the time? We sometimes feel we barely have time to sneak in a few hours' sleep at night. How can we possibly find the time and method for reflection?

Setting a reflection goal and finding a support agent to assist you are key. An excellent resource to begin your journey to quality educational reflection is *The Courage to Teach: A Guide for Reflection and Renewal* by Rachel C. Livsey in collaboration with Parker J. Palmer (2007). This work provides guidelines, a template to follow, and stimulating questions and statements to use as you begin and work to continue reflection. This is written for educators and will provoke thoughtful commentary and rich dialogue. The authors also state that reflection may be individual or group. If you choose group reflection, their guidelines for preparing and creating this reflective environment are excellent.

Reflection could also be a conversation with a peer, some notes scribbled on a Post-it at the end of the day, an entry in your personal journal, or an audio reflection captured on your cell phone. Whether it be a simple or more complex reflection approach, the fact that you're reflecting is the key issue at hand. Thinking and analyzing your daily actions will only strengthen you as a person and teacher.

Build a Learning Community

Learning and growing is much more fun and meaningful when done with others. I was fortunate enough to get my Ph.D. at a university that designed its program around cohort groups. These groups of people began their programs at the same time and had all their classes together. Needless to say, we became quite close and helped each other succeed and survive the program. We learned with and from each other as the program of studies evolved. We combined our intellectual resources to prepare for exams, proficiency tests, and comprehensive assessments. We combined our personalities to make the experience memorable and one that none of us will never forget.

By creating our own learning community, we thrived and grew from our personal and academic interactions. This strengthened our learning adventure. If learning with others would benefit you, see if you can gather a group of coworkers from your school or surrounding schools that might be interested in working together toward a professional goal. Obviously this is easier if you have Professional Learning Communities (PLC) in your school. However, if you do not have one or if yours is not highly functioning, then you might enjoy belonging to a Professional Learning Network (PLN) instead of a PLC. PLNs are addressed in Chapter 14. Either approach can provide you a support network as you learn and grow in a collaborative environment.

> *By creating our own learning community, we thrived and grew from our personal and academic interactions.*

Closing Thoughts

As you have read, renewal can be approached in a wide variety of ways. Find one that is right for you and be in charge of your "refueling journey." Be creative and try something different. As you refill your learning cup, add some delicious cream or sweetener that wasn't there before. You will never regret growing as a person and professional. Becoming a better learner will only make you a better teacher.

8

Celebrating Yourself— You ARE a Professional

> **"***Those who can, teach—
> those who can't, go into some* **"**
> *much less significant line of work.*

Teachers often become so focused on the day-to-day life of their classrooms and schools they forget to celebrate themselves as professionals. They are pulled in many different directions by students, teachers, parents, and administrators. Teachers deserve to feel like the true professionals they are. To feel like a professional often becomes the responsibility of the teacher. There are many ways to celebrate education professionalism. This chapter will suggest a few ways to begin this important celebration. Make these ideas work for you. They could become catalysts for professional development or enhance the evaluation process already in place in your school.

Create Your Professional Portfolio

This wonderful concept allows educators to create a showcase of their goals and accomplishments. The first time I put together my professional portfolio, I dreaded the thought and procrastinated starting. Once I began, you couldn't stop me! It was so much fun pulling together my work and choosing artifacts to be a part of the document. The finished product gave me so much pride that I must have looked through it fifty times the first few days it was done. I used the portfolio as an addition to my résumé in interviews and during evaluation conferences. It has grown and evolved as my professional journey has continued. I now use this yearly in my job evaluation process. That simple act, several years ago, of compiling my teaching achievements has grown into a thorough and complete picture of my professional goals and accomplishments.

Burke (1997) calls this particular portfolio a Career Portfolio. This type of portfolio can be used for job interviews, promotions, and evaluation conferences. It can also simply be a way for educators to capture their teaching journey and serve as a motivating tool, helping them to see how much they have accomplished in their chosen profession. The portfolio becomes a way to collect and record achievements and link these achievements to reflection and professional growth.

Some professionals present their portfolios in hard copy notebook format. This approach allows the document to be easily rearranged and added to, based upon the user's needs. You can also create portfolios using technology. There are many Web 2.0 options to create something of this nature. Some educators even share QR codes to their professional work on their résumé to highlight their technology proficiency.

Organization of your portfolio can be self-determined unless you are creating something for promotion/tenure that would have guidelines decided by your employer. Most schools presently leave this structure open-ended, allowing for individual creativity and focus. One suggested format in Burke (1997) includes the following:

Contents

I. Background information
   A. Updated résumé
   B. Transcript of course work
   C. Philosophy of teaching

D. Teaching goals

E. People who have influenced me

II. Teaching artifacts

A. Recording of or link to your teaching

B. Unit plans

C. Lesson plans

D. Student work samples

E. Reflections on artifacts

F. Assessments

G. Pictures of group projects

H. Recordings of student performances

III. School Improvement

A. Committee work

B. Extracurricular sponsorships

C. Letters to students, parents

D. Letters from students, parents

IV. Professional information

A. Memberships in professional organizations

B. Letters of recommendation

C. Letters of commendation

D. Formal evaluations

E. Awards, certificates (pp. 7–8)

Campbell et al. (1997) has some additional excellent artifact suggestions. Artifacts are pieces of evidence that exhibit the quality of your teaching skills and expertise. They can provide indicators of your teaching competence. Artifact possibilities include anecdotal records, assessments, case studies, classroom management philosophy, computer programs, cooperative learning strategies, curriculum plans, field trip plans, individualized plans, journals, organization strategies, media competencies, meetings and workshop logs, observation reports, peer critiques, pictures and photographs, professional development plans, professional readings list, projects, research papers, schedules, self-assessment instruments, simulated experiences, student contracts, teacher-made materials, theme studies, volunteer experience descriptions, and work experience descriptions.

Another alternative to the binder approach, which can become cumbersome and difficult to reproduce, is an electronic or digital portfolio. Hartnell-Young and Morriss (1999) suggest that a digital portfolio can provide powerful evidence that the teacher is confident with technology and has had the courage to become a learner in the portfolio creation process. This also benefits the students because they have teachers familiar with learning technologies and the teachers can transfer this knowledge into appropriate curriculum activities. Some schools suggest that teachers work in teams to create their individual portfolios. This allows the combined expertise of the group to help all group members and takes away the fear of attempting this project alone.

Portfolio development will help you gain a much clearer picture of yourself as a professional. The process allows for reflection and celebration. The end product will be motivating as you continue your journey toward becoming the complete professional.

Write, Write, and Write Some More!

Writing as a way of professional celebration? Many of you already have your noses turned up indignantly at this notion. I know your time clock is full and I know your engine is already overloaded, but there are many forms of writing that can refuel that engine and share with the world what a quality professional you are.

Many of us read professional journals, blogs, and other online resources to retool, to get new ideas, and to keep up with current trends and research. Who do you think writes the majority of these articles that we read? Teachers *just like you*. They are sharing their thoughts, learning, and ideas with us, and we grow from their writings. You can easily do this too, and it isn't as hard as it may appear. There are many educational journals that want submissions. They request everything from short teaching ideas and stories to longer articles on classroom practice and inquiry. I even had a student in my college course who wrote a touching poem that was printed in a national education periodical.

Starting to write is the hard part. I suggest keeping a journal of short ideas, thoughts, and reflections on teaching for a few weeks. Review the journal and see if there is something in your writing that jumps out at you. You must feel passion and enthusiasm about what you write, and you must have experience to make the content connect with other professionals. If something strikes a chord with you, begin writing your experiences and thoughts in a deeper extension of your original journal entry. See where the writing takes you. Get feedback from peers or coworkers. Seek input and guidance from someone who has been published before. That person can provide great insight and assistance regarding content and where to submit your piece. Remember that there are also state and regional publications looking for articles if you are leery at first of trying a larger national publication.

There are many forms of writing that can refuel that engine and share with the world what a quality professional you are.

Other avenues to begin writing might include starting a personal blog, commenting and reflecting on other people's online commentaries, and utilizing social media options for putting your thoughts into words (see Chapter 14). These small first steps could lead to increased confidence in sharing your perspectives with a larger audience. The formality of social media and online options can vary greatly, but they allow you to venture in at a point where you can feel the most comfortable.

Some of you will find you have a great deal to share and your teacher voice has positive impact through the written word. Writing a book could easily stem from an article or inquiry project in your classroom. Also give thought to writing a book with a colleague. Sharing this experience with someone can provide support and additional ideas. In your quest for a publisher, talk to as many as possible and listen carefully to their suggestions and requirements. Seek out successful authors and listen to their experiences and heed their advice. Your local libraries and institutions of higher learning can be a good starting point.

Share with Colleagues

Know that your knowledge and experience are worth sharing in an oral fashion, too. This can begin with simple dialogue in the faculty workroom and lead to a presentation at a national conference. The first time I went to a state conference, I expected to learn so much from people much smarter than I was because they had been chosen to present. I did learn from some of the presenters, but as I listened to others I realized I knew as much as or more than they did.

You might be amazed how much people would learn from you sharing your theme approach to teaching the Civil War. Think of successful events in your classroom, talk with your peers about some of them, and jot down some of your favorites. Create some notes and overheads. Design a handout and think of creative ways to present your idea to a large group that will involve them in your content. Some principals will encourage staff members to share at faculty meetings. Perhaps you can try your presentation on your colleagues or at a neighboring school. Give it a try! Practice does make perfect. The more you present, the better you will become.

Submit your idea to local, regional, state, or national conference planners. Most of these groups have a formal submission method you can follow. This can sometimes include a description of your presentation, target audience, length of presentation, and audiovisual equipment needed. This method of sharing can be very reinforcing and invigorating. Your feeling of worth at its completion is a true celebration of you as a professional.

Be a Mentor

There are many preservice and beginning teachers that need quality guidance and supervision as they begin their own professional journeys. Sharing your classroom and yourself with them can become a rewarding experience for both parties involved. Sometimes you don't realize how much you have to share until you begin sharing. Your words of wisdom based upon experiences are invaluable for these new teachers. Being a positive role model through your master teaching and interactions with students, colleagues, and parents enrich the knowledge base of teaching interns. Don't be afraid to open your classroom door to them. They are eager to learn and anxious to be with excellent teachers like you.

Correspond Like a Professional

Professionals in the business world have many perks that make them appear professional. You can easily envision high-dollar corporations that have their logo imprinted on everything imaginable. The budgets created in the business of school don't often make allowances for these types of fringe perks because we cannot be frivolous with public money.

Two things you can do for yourself at very little cost are to buy yourself business cards and have some personalized correspondence notes printed. Both of these can be done at local print shops, through catalog mail order venues, or on your computer. You are a professional and you deserve to have business cards to hand out at professional conferences. These cards can also be used during your daily school routine for parents or room visitors. The correspondence cards can have your name, your title

Using something personalized and official looking can make you feel special and can help you remember to celebrate yourself because you ARE a professional.

(Classroom Teacher, Professional Educator, School Counselor, etc.) and the name of the school in which you work. These can be used for parent notes, thank-you notes, and correspondence with other colleagues. Using something personalized and official looking can make you feel special and can help you remember to celebrate yourself because you ARE a professional.

Part III

Raise the Praise—
Minimize the Criticize

9

The Value of Praise

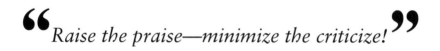

"Raise the praise—minimize the criticize!"

I truly believe that "Raise the praise—minimize the criticize" should not only be the belief system that all educators have at work, but it should be our guiding principle for life. It is critical that we operate from this perspective every day. Consistently taking a positive approach is a central element in establishing and enhancing the morale of others. Looking for, acknowledging, and reinforcing the many positive things that occur in our organization may be the single most essential factor in cultivating positive morale in our organization. This in and of itself is enough of a reason to do it. However, there is even a more compelling one that I will discuss later in the chapter—what your using praise can do for you. Let's take a look at how this belief system got established.

Let's Get Those Kids Lined Up!

My first year as a teacher, I visited an elementary school during the spring. I went over to this K–6 school on a warm Friday afternoon in May. This school was an older building with a simple design. It had one hallway—kind of a shotgun-shaped school. Each grade level had two sections directly across the hall from each other. As you entered the long hallway, first there were two kindergarten classrooms, then two first grades, then two second, etc., down to the two sixth-grade classes. And the teachers were all, at the same time, attempting to have their students line up in that hallway to go to an assembly the students were really excited about attending. Picture for a moment what those "lines" looked like on this warm, Friday afternoon in May. You may be envisioning an amoeba, or a slinky. As you can well imagine, getting those excited students to stand in an orderly fashion was quite a challenge.

I walked into that school by the kindergarten classrooms and was heading toward the far end of the hall. What I heard that day I will never forget. As soon as I walked in the building, I heard the teachers say loudly, "Jimmy, get your hands off Billy!"; threateningly, "Kevin, do you not want to go to the assembly?"; and, with exhaustion, "I've told you at least a dozen times . . ."

You can imagine the lack of impact that this verbal lambasting had. And, every teacher sounded the same and every group of students looked more like a wet noodle than a line. But, out of the corner of my eye, at the far end of the hallway, I saw a sixth-grade class that was lined up straight as an arrow. I remember thinking to myself, "I wonder what that teacher is doing to those kids?" How could she get them in such straight lines? I assumed she must have been a drill sergeant. She had to have been to get the kids lined up so straight. But when I got down to her class I heard something that I have never forgotten. I heard that petite, mild-mannered teacher say, "Susan, I really appreciate the way you are standing so straight and tall and leading our group."; "Johnny, you and Billy are directly behind one another—thank you."; "Jim, you are doing an outstanding job of staying in line." Those students could not wait to hear these words of praise from their teacher.

It is essential that educators constantly work to raise the praise and minimize the criticize, not just some of the time, but in everything they do.

I thought at length about what I had witnessed that day, and then I realized how important it is to consistently emphasize the positive.

It is essential that educators constantly work to raise the praise and minimize the criticize, not just some of the time, but in everything they do. Now, you might be thinking that this positive stuff works for elementary children, but not with middle school students or high school students. And, it especially will not work with college-age people or adults! Well, let's look at an example.

Everybody's Been on a Diet

I have great faith that all of us have been on a diet at one time or another. I now call them "alternative eating plans." Sometimes we have had success and other times we have fallen short of our goals. Usually we start out with great enthusiasm, but often this momentum wanes sooner rather than later. I want you to ask yourself a question. Which is more likely to keep you on a diet? If someone says, "Boy, you are really looking good!" or if someone comments, "It's about time!"

We are never too old to hear praise. Maybe the form needs to be different. We may be conscious of what others think when we get recognized, but it still feels good. When was the last time that someone told you or gave you a note that said how much you are appreciated? If you can remember, do you recall how good you felt? Did that make you work harder or slack off? Of course, it gave you a real boost. Realizing this can help us to focus on raising the praise. After all, we have all been on a diet.

Five Things That Help Praise Work

One of the challenges that all educators face is learning how to praise. That may seem silly, but often teachers have spent their whole careers looking for what is wrong, pointing out errors, and focusing on mistakes. This is a part of being an educator. However, an exceptional teacher looks for opportunities to find people doing things right. One of the difficulties for many educators is truly understanding praise and being able to apply it on a daily basis.

Ben Bissell (1992) has described five things that help praise work. He feels that these are important elements in order for praise attempts to have the most positive effect possible. The five things Dr. Bissell indicates as characteristics of effective praise are *authentic, specific, immediate, clean,* and *private.* Let us apply these general characteristics to the specifics of motivating and praising in our daily lives.

Authentic means that we are praising people for something genuine, recognizing them for something that is true. This is an important facet because the recognition of something authentic can never grow weary. Sometimes people state that they do not praise more because they feel that it will lose its credibility or that it will become less believable if it happens too much. The way to prevent this is to make sure that it is always authentic. No one ever complains of being praised too much for something genuine. Authentic does not mean that it is earth-shattering or that it is a magnificent accomplishment. Instead, the only requirement is that it be true. We do not need to wait until someone loses 55 pounds before we compliment that person. We don't mind hearing we are looking good even at the end of the first week of our diet! As educators, we have many opportunities to catch people doing things right. Remembering and sharing them with the person you are praising is an important facet of praising.

The second characteristic of effective praise is *specific*. The behavior we acknowledge often becomes the behavior that will be continued. If we can recognize others' positive efforts with specific recognition, then we can help them see specific areas of value. For example, acknowledging that a student did an effective job of asking questions during a class period can help reinforce the specific actions that were done correctly. Specific praise also allows you to reinforce someone in an authentic manner. If you use specific praise, you can recognize everyone in your classes. Even students that are struggling can still be praised. You do not have to be dishonest and say they are outstanding students academically, or that a paper was excellent if it wasn't. Instead, you can identify those areas that did have merit and acknowledge them through praise.

> **The behavior we acknowledge often becomes the behavior that will be continued.**

I am reminded of a student named Aaron who was walking down the hallway one February day. I was principal at the time and I noticed Aaron had a new sweater on. The reason I knew it was a new sweater was because Aaron was one of those students that I saw often enough so that I pretty much knew his entire wardrobe. As Aaron got near I said to him, "Boy Aaron, that is a good-looking sweater you've got on there." Not only did Aaron crack a smile, but he wore that sweater to school every day for the next three weeks! Finally I had to get to his physical education class to compliment him on his P.E. clothes just to get him to wear something else!

The third item is *immediate*. This means recognizing positive efforts and contributions in a timely manner. Providing authentic and specific feedback in close proximity to when it occurs is an important element in making reinforcement effective. We are so fortunate in education. We have dozens of opportunities every day to give immediate feedback to those around us. We can compliment a student on effort, a peer on helping others, or anyone on wearing a nice shirt. Doing this in an expedient fashion can help the idea of praise becoming much more of a habit.

> *Providing authentic and specific feedback in close proximity to when it occurs is an important element in making reinforcement effective.*

The fourth guideline for praise is *clean*. This is often a very challenging requirement for praise. The expectation that praise be clean is especially challenging for educators. Clean means a couple of different things.

The first is that praise is not clean if you are issuing it in order to get someone to do something in the future. In other words, it is important to compliment someone because it is authentic, not just because you are hoping that the person will do something different tomorrow. This is an area that is important to remind yourself of quite regularly. Because if you do not, you will be tempted to discontinue praising because you will feel it "did not work." An example of this would be if you praise a student about the good job done on homework that day and then two weeks later that student does not turn in an assignment. Do not feel that these two events are linked. Oftentimes we take the unprofessional actions of less positive students and adults very personally. Though our goal is to get them to be more positive, we need to be aware that more often their mood has much more to do with them and the way they feel about themselves, than it does with you and how they regard you.

The second element of clean praise is a very challenging one for educators. This requirement is for reinforcement to be clean, it cannot include the word "but." If we are trying to compliment someone and we say, "I appreciated the work you did on your math today, but you need to finish your social studies assignment," the individual we hoped we were praising will very likely only remember the part after the "but," which was a criticism. The student will be very unlikely to recall the attempted compliment regarding math. If we are really meaning to praise someone, then it is important that we separate these two events. If we could have stopped with, "I appreciated the work you did on your math today," then this could have been an authentic, specific, immediate, positive, and reinforcing event for this student. This helps establish two things. It helps clarify and reinforce the expectations you have for the manner in which students should complete work. It also makes it much more likely that the student will more consciously seek to repeat this behavior in this manner in the future. The other part of the comment may not have a need for immediacy. Tying these two together reduces or even eliminates the value of the praise. Building the morale of others requires a consistent focus on looking for positive things. Anytime the opportunity presents itself, acknowledging it appropriately can continue to cultivate a positive mind-set among others.

Let's think back to the diet example. If I tell someone, "You really look like you have lost weight, but what has happened to your hair?" this person will remember this conversation being much more about hair than about weight loss.

The fifth descriptor of praise is *private*. Dr. Bissell believes that the vast majority of the time, praise needs to be in private. I agree with this and would also say that if in doubt, you are always safe to praise someone in private. Remember the old days when teachers would say, "I am giving back the tests from best to worst. Jimmy come on up and get yours first." Often the end result of this is that either Jimmy makes sure he never gets the best grade again, or the other students make sure that they take out their frustration on Jimmy at recess or in the lunchroom.

This same concept of public versus private praising is applicable to students throughout the school. Recognizing students publicly when they get a 3.5 GPA may seem reinforcing, but many of these students would rather receive private recognition because it may not be "cool" to have accomplished it. Realistically, we often have many students in our schools who could not have achieved this lofty GPA. Having a private ceremony for these 3.5 students, or sending their parents a letter, would probably accomplish this same thing without potentially building resentment among their peers. However you elect to reinforce the efforts of others, it is essential that you "Raise the Praise!" on a regular basis.

Practicing the Praise

Praise is valuable in that it can assist others. However, maybe even more importantly, it is also a powerful tool that can reinforce the praiser. When I was an assistant principal, I realized that it was up to me whether or not I was going to enjoy my job. If I just waited around for things to happen, they surely would. Unfortunately, most of the things that come the way of an assistant principal responsible for discipline of 750 eighth graders tend to be negative. I realized that I was going to deal with students when they were in trouble, teachers when they had a problem, and parents when they were upset. I then determined that it was my responsibility to structure my job so that it would be enjoyable to come to work each day. In order to try to maintain a little balance in my job, I started a positive referral program.

Most schools have discipline referrals, where teachers "write up" kids for misbehavior and then send them to the office with the referral form. Assistant principals often deal with the majority of these situations. However, I felt that it was important to have a positive referral program. This was a form that was similar in format, only we put it on bright red paper. Teachers would "write up" students for doing positive things. It could be that Tim got a B+ on a math quiz, they enjoy seeing Megan's smiling face every day, or that Juan helped a student who was on crutches move around the school for a week. As long as it was something authentic, it was appropriate to write up a positive referral and put it in my mailbox.

When I pulled the positive referral out of my mailbox, I would send for the student. Initially, students were nervous, frightened, or defensive when they were summoned to the office. Often students would walk in and immediately tell the secretary, "It wasn't me!" When I called the students into my office, I would first congratulate them and tell them how proud I was of their accomplishment. I would share with them which teacher referred them and why he or she did so. I would thank them for their contribution to making our school a better place.

Praise is valuable in that it can assist others. However, maybe even more importantly, it is also a powerful tool that can reinforce the praiser.

This, in and of itself, may have been enough. However, I took it one step further. I would pick up the phone and call the child's parent. And, if the child lived with two parents, I would call the one that worked. And, if both parents worked, I would call the one that worked in the busiest office or on the most crowded factory assembly line. Let's think for a moment what those phone calls were like. Here is an example that involves calling Kenny Johnson's mother at work for a positive referral. "Hi. Mrs. Johnson, this is Bill Smith, assistant principal at Meadow Grove Middle School."

As you can imagine, this conversation was usually interrupted at this point by the parent with a loud moan, "Oh, no!" I would then continue with the conversation. "Mrs. Johnson, I hate to bother you at work, but I just thought you might want to know that Kenny's teacher, Mrs. Jones, is running around up here at school, bragging about your son. She sent me a positive referral saying that Kenny did an excellent job working with his group leading a science experiment yesterday. I called Kenny down to the office to congratulate him and I wanted to call and share the good news with you."

The conversation then would typically continue in a very positive manner and I would let the parent know that the student was in the office with me and that the parent was welcome to talk with the child.

A lot of principals have positive referrals and other programs in their schools. This is wonderful. However, the added twist of calling the parents at work led to several significant and positive contributions for me. Interestingly, the most frequent comment I received from parents was, "A school has never called with anything good before." This was consistently the theme when I called hundreds and hundreds of parents. It did not matter if I was contacting the parent of a student who was frequently in trouble or the future valedictorian. Parents had never had unsolicited, positive contact from anyone at school.

Though I thought this was very sad, it did help me realize a couple of things. First, I finally understood why people believe the criticism of schools and teachers they read in the newspapers. I now was also able to comprehend why people buy into the nonsense that they hear on radio call-in shows criticizing educators and schools in America. If they do not hear good news from us, the public may never hear good news about schools and teachers. Thus, it is critically important that we consistently initiate positive contact with parents.

At this point you may be asking yourself a couple of things. "Why did you call parents specifically at work?" and "This is all fine, but what does this have to do with building personal morale?" Well, let me take a stab at both of those questions.

I called the parents at work for a very selfish reason. It relates to the publicity issue. When I called Mrs. Johnson and her initial reaction was a loud, "Oh, no!," do you have any guess what was the first thing she did in that crowded office when she hung up the phone? She told everybody in the office! I also know there was an office full of other parents who were thinking to themselves that their child's school never has called with good news. Anything that builds the reputation of your school only helps the morale of everyone in the building.

Just imagine the impact on the relationship between the teacher who wrote the referral and the student who was referred. So many times, the student would go into the classroom the next day and thank the teacher. The student would describe excitedly that the parent was so happy to hear the news and took the family out for pizza. What a positive impact this had on teacher-student relations. The relationship between the teacher and the parents was also greatly enhanced.

Additionally, there were some benefits involved in this whole process for me. One of them was if I had to call the parent at some future point with less than good news, I received a positive response from the parent. If I had previously initiated positive contact with a parent, it was amazing how that impacted future calls. Let's pretend we have to call Mrs. Johnson several weeks later over a discipline matter.

"Hi. Mrs. Johnson, this is Bill Smith, assistant principal at Meadow Grove Middle School."

And Mrs. Johnson would reply, "Hi. How are you today?"

At first, I would be so shocked by Mrs. Johnson's friendly response that I would assume she had not understood me! But, eventually I would continue . . .

"Mrs. Johnson, I hate to bother you at work, but today Kenny was involved in an incident where he . . . (was fighting, sent to the office, etc.) and as a result he will be receiving . . . (detention, suspension, etc.)"

Mrs. Johnson would say, "That's okay. I know you're fair. You call me with good news and you call me with bad news. You can call me anytime you want."

What I quickly learned was that making positive referrals may have seemed like additional work, but it really made my job easier. I had built relationships with parents that had significant positive impacts down the line. My job just became more tolerable. However, the real benefit from making positive phone calls was even more selfish. Let's examine the most powerful result of these positive phone calls. After making positive phone calls for two years as an assistant, we had such a positive response from students, parents, and the community (even the newspaper wrote about it!) that the teachers decided to get personally involved. The teaching staff, when I became principal, decided that each teacher would make one positive phone call per week.

It is essential that we realize that all of us can do this on our own. We can decide that once or twice a week we will make it our number one priority to call a parent with words of praise about his or her child. No matter what the age, we never get too old to hear positive things about those we love. Our schools do not need a structured program or incentive. We can do it because it makes things more enjoyable for our students, but also, it gives us a boost every time we do it!

Remembering the Praise

One of the biggest challenges we face is to remember to praise. If we can take a more selfish approach, which might seem ironic because we are talking about praise, it may allow it to be more enduring. As a school, we realized that we needed to dedicate a day to this. Because as all of us know, if we do not choose a particular day and write it down in our calendars and/or lesson plan books, we will most likely forget. So, we chose Tuesday and we called it "Terrific Tuesday." So, rather than struggling to remember to praise, write it in your lesson plan book and/or your calendars. You will be glad you did.

I want to return to the selfish interest in making positive referral phone calls or utilizing any type of praise. We determine how much we praise. We are all aware of that. Now, I want us to ask a question. Any time we praise, at least how many people feel better? The answer, of course, is two. And, one of those two people is always yourself. In other words, anytime we praise, we feel better!

As a matter of fact, according to Ben Bissell (1992), the single biggest determinant of how much we praise is how we feel about ourselves. That is why we devote a chapter of this book to the importance of praising. Remember, if we do not take care of ourselves, there is not much chance we can take care of anyone else either.

Rather than struggling to remember to praise, write it in your lesson plan book and/or your calendars. You will be glad you did.

One of the best ways to build personal morale is to praise others. In other words, one thing you can do any time you want to feel better at work (or anywhere else, for that matter) is to praise someone else. The result is amazing. Not only do you help someone else to feel better, you feel better as well! And the most valuable aspect is the positive cycle you can start with yourself. Every time you praise, you feel better. And, the better you feel, the more you praise! Now that is the kind of rut I want to get into at work and at home.

What do we do if someone we praise doesn't receive it in the manner we would like, or maybe even responds negatively? The answer is nothing. We don't change a thing we are doing. We have to make sure that we do not give negative people the power to ruin a great idea. Chapter 13 goes into greater detail on the idea of not giving power to negative people around us, but it is important at this point to make sure that we do not let them spoil our fun.

Find a Way That Works for You!

Maybe instead of phone calls, or maybe in addition, you acquire a supply of postcards. The postcards can be bright and cheery. Around the outside border they can say, "Great job, Way to go, Terrific, Outstanding, Excellent," etc. You can fill one out regarding a student and then mail it to the student's home. Other options could include personal e-mails, classroom tweets, and posting student work or project pictures on classroom Web pages, school Facebook sites, or other school-approved online locations.

Every teacher has numerous ways to praise others. The key to building personal morale is to consistently recognize the efforts of everyone you come in contact with by modeling the praising for all to see. This approach is contagious in any organization. So, take care of yourself, have fun, and raise the praise!

10

Making School Work for You

> **“**We make a living by what we get,
> but we make a life by what we give.**”**
>
> —*Sir Winston Churchill*

There are many day-to-day activities that occur in the school that you can use to benefit the health of your mind and body. Some of these activities we do in a rote fashion and don't think about how the activity can benefit us. Others are perhaps hidden and need to be discovered and used. Try them out. Each person is different and what works for some might not work for others. Experiment and always be on the lookout for additional ways the school environment can benefit you. This chapter focuses on the events and people in the school who can support your well-being.

Hall/Playground Duty

Traditionally, many of us dread these duties. Well, you must do them, so why not make the best of it? Hall duty is often seen as the time to watch for trouble, keep a tight rein on students, and bark out commands as the students pass. Why not view hall duty as the opportunity to build rapport with students, smile at them, and find ways to praise positive behavior? If this becomes your approach, you will end hall duty in a better frame of mind and make some great connections with students. These connections could pay off in classroom behaviors down the road.

Why not view hall duty as the opportunity to build rapport with students, smile at them, and find ways to praise positive behavior?

Playground duty is another example of mind over matter. You can use this time to walk around talking to groups of children, asking questions, and maybe joining in their game for a few moments. Create a climate of calm control and show them you have a human side, too. You can blow the whistle at the end of duty with a smile on your face and eliminate the recess headache.

Physical Education

Have you ever considered joining the P.E. class? Give it some thought. The class often is doing activities you would enjoy, the children would see you in another learning setting, and you would have a great opportunity to participate in some healthy activities.

Some schools also have weight rooms with bikes and treadmills. You can utilize these rooms before or after school and get your workout finished at your place of employment for free!

Greeting Students in the Morning

This really is a wonderful way to start your teaching day. Greet them as they get off buses, stand at the front door, or just make sure you are at the classroom door to let all of them know how glad you are that they are at school today. Smile, say the child's name, and share positive comments about the upcoming day. You will feel great and so will your students.

Media Centers

These areas have really become the heart of schools and offer so many resources to teachers. Of course, there are books, books, and more books. This vast supply of quality literature at your fingertips is invaluable.

The media specialist is there to help you, as well as the students. Let this person assist you in locating appropriate references, specific titles, and collections for research. Solicit opinions on new books that have arrived and suggest new titles for the library to purchase.

Use the periodical section in the media center. Many schools subscribe to periodicals you may be receiving at home. When budgets become tight at home, know that many current newspapers and magazines will be available for you to use in your school's media center. Also remember that the more you use the media center, the more you are modeling for your students the importance of the center and how much it can offer. Your actions often speak louder than your words.

Coworkers and Colleagues

Many of your peers have talents and knowledge to offer. Keep your eyes and ears open. You will become aware of each person's individual talents and areas of expertise. Some staff members love to create crafts, others have musical talents to offer, while someone else might be an expert in understanding car engines. Everyone's outside interests and talents could benefit you at some time. In turn, make sure everyone knows what your talents are and that you are willing to share them.

The School Secretary

I cannot emphasize enough the importance of establishing a positive relationship with this person, who should be treated with dignity and respect. The secretary has a difficult job and juggles multiple tasks constantly. If you have a productive, working relationship with the secretary, it can often make your day smoother. The secretary can ensure that you get messages at appropriate times, provides extra copies of forms you lost, and makes sure you are not interrupted unnecessarily during class. This person can become a key player in your daily sanity. Work hard at this relationship and nurture its continued growth.

The Custodian

This is another key player in your daily success. The custodian should be treated with respect and with the same regard as your grade-level coworkers. Like the secretaries, custodians' jobs are important and demanding. Thank them for their efforts and greet them each day. These small tokens of appreciation will mean so much and help you establish a working relationship with them.

The School Nurse

The school nurse's primary job is the wellness of students, but also to assist you with health-related questions and concerns. The nurse certainly cannot replace your doctor or write prescriptions, but can give advice and suggestions on health-related issues. The nurse must stay up-to-date on current health care trends and can be a wonderful resource in these areas.

"Must Have" Files

As we focus on ways to make your life easier and more productive, here are some simple suggestions for "must have" files. These are files that can help make your day run smoother, which in turn keeps you happier and more productive.

1. *Attaboy/Attagirl*. This was mentioned in Chapter 6, but it is worth mentioning again. This file is your collection of notes, letters, and documents that have become a tribute to your work as a teacher. Make sure you retain these items, and pull them out for reading periodically. They can help you remember just why you chose this profession and give you a morale boost.

2. *Fun Ideas*. This is exactly what the name says. This file is a collection of fun and creative teaching ideas that can be implemented quickly and easily into your classroom structure. Pull out this file on days when you feel like you're not connecting with the students or not enjoying teaching. One or two of these ideas implemented in your lesson could be exactly the energy boost you need.

3. *Inspirational Stories and Quotes*. In the teaching profession, we often come across stories and quotations that provide us thoughtful reflection and motivation. Collect these and pull them out when you need a jump start. Share them with coworkers and pass along positive energy!

4. *Emergency Folder*. This folder contains generic lesson plans for a substitute teacher that could be implemented easily. You may become so sick you cannot come in to prepare lesson plans for a sub. It will ease your mind to know that you have a plan to fall back on if this becomes the case. This folder contains schedules, class lists, emergency procedures, and lesson plans for each subject.

Find ways to make the school environment work for you. Open your eyes to the possibilities and search for ways to make your life as an educator easier. The school environment can be productive for you, but you must become proactive in searching for routes to this productivity. You give so much of yourself to the school. Why not allow it to return the favor?

Unexpected Happiness

"*Good things come in small packages.*"

This is the shortest chapter in this book. Always keep in mind that it's quality, not quantity. I feel confident that although the length is minimal, the personal satisfaction you'll feel from using this chapter will be enormous.

We all enjoy receiving presents and there are times when we expect them, such as birthdays, holidays, anniversaries, etc. Think about the present you received from someone for no apparent reason or "just because." My guess is that the gesture meant a lot because that person wasn't giving you a gift in recognition of some preplanned event. It was unexpected and given to you because someone really cared. I call this an Unexpected Happiness. Have you ever given someone an Unexpected Happiness? If you have, you are aware that two people feel very good when this occurs. Of course, the person at the receiving end is thrilled and touched. The wonderful part is that the giver is equally, or sometimes more, fulfilled than the receiver.

There are an infinite amount of ways to spread the Unexpected Happiness cheer throughout your school and professional work day. I have begun the list for you. We have even added a blank page for you to continue this list as you discover ways to make people feel good, while making yourself feel good, too. Enjoy your task, and may the giving of Unexpected Happiness provide you with Unexpected Happiness!

Unexpected Happiness List

♦ Take your morning cup of coffee outside and greet students as they get off the bus.

♦ Bring doughnuts for your coworkers "just because."

♦ Help the custodian empty trash cans during your part of your break.

♦ Drop a thank-you note to a coworker for being there for you each day. Keep notecards handy for spontaneous note writing to anyone in the school.

♦ Leave a big, bright, shiny apple on your principal's desk one morning.

♦ Bring flowers for the secretary.

♦ Head out to recess and play kickball. Yes, play, not supervise!

♦ Take over the crossing guard's duty after school and give the guard the afternoon off.

♦ Ride a bus route and get to know the driver.

♦ Give restaurant gift certificates to the teachers who cook so they won't have to cook! Get some coworkers to pitch in with you and cut your costs.

♦ Take time to thank people verbally for their efforts. Look them in the eye, take your time, and make them know you really mean what you say.

♦ Invite the new teacher to go out for coffee and conversation after school one day.

♦ If you find a great joke or cartoon, send a copy to others and brighten their day.

♦ Ask your coworker about his son's soccer game last night.

- Notice new haircuts.
- Cover someone else's class during your plan period.
- Anonymously buy the custodian's lunch.
- Write a note to a teacher that influenced your education.
- Tell three teachers that you wish your child was in their class.
- Help chip off ice on the front steps on snowy days.
- Park at the far end of the lot to allow others to be closer to the school.
- Say hi to every student you see in the hall during the day—it might be important to them.
- Take another teacher's tray back to the cafeteria when you take yours.
- Bring a pound of flavored coffee to share with everyone.
- Send surprise Christmas cards to the parents of your students.
- Buy the new teacher a staff T-shirt.
- Supply munchies at the next faculty meeting.
- Stay late for a week and offer tutoring to students who are interested.
- Call parents just to tell them how much you enjoy having their son/daughter in your class.

Remember, this list is only the beginning. The possibilities are endless. Use the following page to add ideas and continue to spread Unexpected Happiness.

Unexpected Happiness List

Your List

1. _____
2. _____
3. _____
4. _____
5. _____
6. _____
7. _____
8. _____
9. _____
10. _____
11. _____
12. _____

12

Your Home Away from Home

> " *There's no place like home.* "
> —*Dorothy in* The Wizard of Oz

Think about the number of hours you spend at work. I'm sure most of you spend seven to ten hours per day at your workplace. This doesn't include the nights and weekends you put in extra hours to finish projects and prepare your teaching plans. If you are going to spend this much time in one place, then the place should be comfortable, inviting, and easy to work in. Creation of this kind of environment is within your control. It doesn't entail spending a lot of money or even buying new furniture. You can take what you have and create a work atmosphere that invites you in and makes the daily tasks you must complete seem less overwhelming.

At one time, my own office was a case in point. It was a renovated dorm room and was built with efficiency in mind, not comfort. The concrete walls and metal shelving did not exude any warmth or comfort, but I was not to be denied an office that welcomed me each day! Some cheery curtains, a plush rug, cushions for the chairs, pictures on the walls, and some silk flowers quickly made it a place I wanted to come into each day. I also did my best to keep things shelved, put away, and filed. When I enter my office and it is in order, I am much more productive. I am not depressed by the clutter and piles of "mystery" correspondence and handouts. I know what needs to be done and am not distracted by an office in disarray.

Let's translate all of this to the place we call school. Whitaker (1997) found that in schools with a more positive climate, the atmosphere was orderly, warm, and inviting. Most of you can probably picture these schools. These are the schools in which you enter and can feel good without having to talk to anyone. You know what the school stands for and can tell it is student centered. You want people to get a strong sense of the personality of your school as they walk up the front steps and enter the doors. Once inside, the climate of the school should be visibly evident. The foyer should be welcoming as well as the office area. The physical presence of the school should portray the climate and personality of the students and staff within.

One exercise I do with my preservice teachers is called a "climate hunt." The building where we have class has fifteen floors. Each floor houses a different department and has an entrance foyer that people travel through to get to offices. Some floors have foyers that are cheery and welcoming. Others look institutional and barren. The preservice students are instructed to travel to different floors, not speaking to anyone as they move from level to level. They are to take notes on how they feel and their first impressions on the various floors. They return to class and we discuss their findings. They speak of feeling "welcome, excited, and inspired" on the floors with attractive entrances. In turn, they share their feelings of "despair, depression, and sadness" when they visit the floors with little visual interest. We then discuss which floors we might like to work on and why. Naturally, they all choose to work on the floors that feel welcoming. They say that the "upbeat tone, positive feel, and purposeful design" would make them feel comfortable and entice them to desire working in these places. We discuss how our classrooms must be designed to create warm and inspiring climates for our students. "Upbeat, positive, and purposeful" are some of the exact words we would like to use when describing our own classroom atmosphere.

This simple activity helps us see the power of the look and feel of the building you work in and how this can affect the attitude and morale of the people who work there. You want to be uplifted when you walk in, you want to feel comfortable, and you want to be inspired to do your very best work while in the school. Spending time on your physical environment is time well spent, not only for you, but also for the students, parents, and community.

It Can Start with One Person

When I became a principal, I was fortunate enough to become the administrator of a building that, overall, had a dedicated and bright staff. These teachers had worked hard on curriculum building and instructional pedagogy for the past four years. There was a very solid foundation that had been built. As I looked around and wondered where to begin, I could tell that the physical environment was clean and orderly but lacked that warm and inviting appeal you want a building to have. In one of my administrator preparation courses, we visited a school that exuded a positive climate all over the building. From the minute we walked into the building that day, our sense of comfort and invigoration was established. The day was spent observing, talking to teachers, interacting with students, and conversing with the principal. After seeing and "feeling" the school, we all left so motivated and inspired. I began to ponder how I could make a school look and feel this way. My task began as a solo pursuit, but soon turned into a building-wide effort.

During the summer before I began my first year, I spent time transforming the lounge and the outer office. I painted, stenciled, and organized bulletin boards. Fortunately the springs were sticking out of the lounge furniture, thus enabling me to plead for some new comfortable pieces for the staff. We stenciled the office, added some prints I made out of old calendar pictures and inexpensive frames, and popped a silk floral arrangement on the counter. A crafty parent took a large grapevine wreath and hot glued "school" items on it. She placed pencils, markers, rulers, pens, a box of crayons, scissors, etc., on the wreath and topped it with a bow made from ribbon with bright red apples on it. We hung this in front of the office as a welcome signal to all who entered. I also added a wooden bench in front of the office and placed a table next to it with flowers on it. Then we spent time making the faculty restroom a little less bland. A little paint, some shelving, pictures, attractive towels, a rug, and some material velcroed to the sink as a skirt to cover cleaning supplies added an "executive" touch to a once drab and institutional restroom.

It was also interesting how these changes began to have a domino effect with the faculty and staff. The custodian and secretary joined in the fun as they began to notice the uplifting results. When the staff arrived, they began to take notice and before I knew it they were volunteering their talents by sewing, painting, and stenciling. Once everyone was back and began to see the transformations, there began to be informal conversations about how these changes could be continued into other parts of the school. I told the staff about the school I visited, and we decided to take van-loads of teachers there to observe. Most of the faculty were able to see the school and came back with many wonderful ideas. These ideas and many additional ones will be shared in this chapter.

Remember that this transformation began with one person setting the stage for change in a nonthreatening way. I have seen the same thing happen when one teacher tries something new and catches the attention of the other teachers. A classroom teacher told me the story about a new teacher who moved into her building. This teacher had been working diligently on creating a warm and inviting climate in her room. Her final touches were some beautiful plants purchased at a local hardware store. They really make the room come alive. Word spread quickly down the hall and soon everyone came to her classroom and wanted to know where she got the plants, how many were left, and how long would they be on sale.

You might be amazed by the change you can stimulate when you focus on your personal teaching/learning environment.

Needless to say, that group of teachers bought out the store and luscious green plants greeted all the students in that hallway on the first day of school . . . the power of one person.

My work began as small projects in the office and lounge and eventually spread throughout the entire school. Your work could begin in your own classroom and you might be amazed by the change you can stimulate when you focus on your personal teaching/learning environment. Some staff will be more enthusiastic than others, but that is fine. Just remember, any improvement is movement in the right direction and better than where you began. Just take it project by project, and enjoy your small successes along the way.

Classrooms

You can begin with your own classroom—the place where you spend seven to ten hours each day. Make this place one you enjoy entering each day. If you feel good walking in, it will positively affect your teaching attitude and mentality.

Teachers are so creative and are masters at discovering endless possibilities for everything! After I took my staff to visit the school with a positive climate, they began such a wonderful transformation of their own classrooms. I watched more painting and stenciling than I could ever imagine. There were pale yellow walls with stenciled apples and light blue walls with stenciled dinosaurs. I began to see plants, rocking chairs, lamps, curtains, beanbag chairs, aquariums, rugs, couches, and even lofts appear throughout the building. Clutter and messy areas began to disappear. Student work was displayed more often, mobiles began to hang from the ceilings, and a student-made quilt was prepared for exhibit in the entrance hallway. The teachers and students worked very hard making their classrooms feel more homey and inviting.

Teachers also learn where to go for the bargains that will help improve school climate. Many stores give away their seasonal posters and displays when they are finished with them. Don't be afraid to ask for these items. They might say no, but they more often say yes! While walking through a bookstore one day, I saw some wonderful posters of children reading. I asked about them and the manager said to come back in a couple of weeks to pick them up. After getting the posters, I laminated them and these posters adorned our hallways during National Library Week. I sent a thank-you note to the bookstore owner with a picture of the cheery hallways he had helped create with his donation. One teacher noticed her child's day-care throwing out some colorful rugs. She asked for them and was loading the rugs in her van within minutes. We cleaned and vacuumed them, then they were placed in our kindergarten and first-grade classrooms. One of my reading teachers found a vinyl couch at Salvation Army. She cleaned it up, added some throw pillows, and moved it into her classroom. I can still see her on that couch, all nestled in, reading with her students.

Another simple climate element is music. Feel free to play soft music while students are working independently or during indoor recess time. Music can have a calming effect on all ages, from young children to adults, and it is an opportunity to introduce various styles of music to children. One of my favorites to hear in the classroom is classical music. Many children do not hear this music on a regular basis and the exposure is healthy for them. I will never forget watching a first-grade classroom come in from recess. They were quite wound up as most first graders are

Music has a place in every classroom and can add an interesting ambiance to learning environments.

after recess. The teacher had soft, classical music playing as they entered the room. You could just see their bodies relax and they began to speak quietly as they calmly began their next academic task. Music has a place in every classroom and can add an interesting ambiance to learning environments.

It is a good idea is to keep a basket of toys and books in your classroom for visits in which younger siblings accompany the parent. These toys can help keep the child entertained so you and the parent can converse with minor interruption. Parents will appreciate your thoughtfulness, and you will value the quality meeting time with them.

We can all picture wonderful classrooms where entering and staying is pure pleasure. I encourage you to create these magical settings in each of your learning environments. It will inspire you daily as you work to inspire your students.

With the blessing and support of your principal, you might be interested in enhancing other areas of your building. Some schools have climate committees for this purpose alone. The following sections provide some ideas for other areas of the school.

The Entrance Doors and Foyer

Make sure that your entrance is well-maintained and welcoming. Keep doors painted and glass cleaned. Include a sign that welcomes visitors to your school and politely requests them to check in at the office. One principal told me he placed a sign on the door that read, "Please come to the office so we can warmly welcome you." He used this wording purposefully. He said, "If those words are there, then we have to be sure we are doing it!"

Once inside the doors, use the foyer to set the tone for the rest of the building. Display children's work, paint a mural, use plants, and/or include attractive benches if possible. Many schools display their mission statements professionally framed, so that all can see the true purpose of their school. One school even has a couple of rocking chairs in the foyer with a basket of books on a table between them. This helps bide time for mothers waiting with young children and serves as a wonderful reading area for volunteers to work with students.

This area is an integral "first impression" spot. Many people will form their opinion of the school based upon the feeling they have in the first few minutes they enter the building. Continuously monitor this area so it is not neglected. Make sure it is clean, attractive, and welcoming. You can also have a PTA committee that is responsible for "entrance appearance." Empowering an interested group of parents can assure that the first impression that students, staff, and visitors see each day is dynamic. Assigning the appearance of different parts of the school to different groups is a way to "spread the wealth" and help schoolwide pride infiltrate throughout the school. There is a middle school that does this by advisory group, but rotates the areas each month. One advisory group has the foyer, one the cafeteria, each hallway is assigned, etc. Then, these get rotated regularly so that every student and staff member has some ownership of the entire building.

The School Office

This is another area where first impressions are made. Probably one of the most important elements that should be present in the office is the smile and warm greeting of the school secretary, teacher, or principal. This costs no money and can reap great rewards. I'll never forget the feeling I got the time I entered a school office and the secretary was on the phone. She and a friend were discussing last night's football game and how unruly the students were. She knew I was there, yet kept her conversation going, initiating even more banter about the students' behaviors. I tried not to listen, but it was impossible. I looked around the office for a place to sit. There were a couple of chairs shoved in a corner, so I sat down. The chair I chose was unstable, so I looked at the other one. It was so dirty, I didn't want to move. There were piles of dust in the corners on the floor and a couple of wilted plants on the counter. While I was sitting there, another staff member walked through the office. He looked at me, frowned, and walked away. Finally the principal came out of his office and asked if he could help me. I replied that I was there for an appointment with him and followed him into his private office. The secretary's conversation still droned on. Needless to say, this first impression was quite negative. Even though the office appearance was neglected, the secretary's behavior was what really stuck in my mind. If she would have been professional enough to greet me, smile, and conclude her phone conversation, the neglected office wouldn't have seemed so pitiful.

The first words spoken to visitors and the manner in which they are spoken set a powerful tone for these important guests. As a teacher, model this appropriate behavior and help handle situations in a pleasant and professional way, especially when students are present. Students' ears hear everything and they usually can't wait to get home or back to the classroom to share their overheard "news."

The office area should be attractive and orderly. Fresh paint, plants, and pictures take little time and can add so much to a significantly visible area of your school. An elementary school I recently spent some time in had a border of colorful handprints around the office. When I asked about it, the principal told me that every student in the school had his or her handprint somewhere in the building. This was also done in the cafeteria and hallways.

One high school I visited had added a simple wallpaper border around the office and professionally framed student artwork on the walls. Numerous cushioned chairs were available to sit in and educational magazines were set out on an attractive end table topped with a table lamp. The look was professional, clean, and comfortable. I was greeted by a warm smile and a secretary who made me feel at home immediately. These were simple additions to the office, but ones that set a positive tone and sent a welcoming message to visitors, community, staff, and students.

The Staff Lounge

This is a place where everyone can enjoy the fruits of his or her labors and will appreciate the attention and interest in supplying comfort. Sprucing up the staff lounge is a great morale booster and can be as simple as creating usable, attractive bulletin boards. I went to a brand-new school recently where the staff lounge was filled with new furniture and a lovely kitchenette. This wonderful facility lacked warmth and interest. The bulletin boards were barren and the walls were drab. There was excellent shelving for what might have been a professional resource center, but I couldn't really tell what was on the shelves. It seemed to be a clutter of books and magazines with no evident purpose. No one had given this area the attention it needed and deserved. Just some cheery bulletin board greetings and an organized resource center would have added so much to this lounge, entailing a little time and effort.

I have seen lounges where the school leaders have taken the time to make them places where staff members can relax, converse, and share a cup of morning coffee. These spaces are filled with comfortable furniture, flowers on the tables, bulletin boards with purpose, window treatments, rugs or carpeted areas, and inspirational pictures or posters on the walls. A comfortable and relaxing haven can give many teachers inspiration and the opportunity for renewal throughout the day. Some schools keep chalkboards or dry erase boards in the lounges for quick staff updates or uplifting quotes. Bulletin boards can be organized into sections providing a variety of information to staff. One section can be used to share flyers for upcoming workshops and conferences, one can be used for district information, and another can post your weekly staff memo, the lunch menu, the school newsletter, etc. Teachers will appreciate having this information for easy referral during break or lunch conversations. Some lounges also house professional resources (books, magazines, and DVDs). I know one principal that highlights one resource each week. He displays it on the top of the resource bookcase with a short written "book talk" sharing important and interesting aspects of the book. This keeps teachers aware of what's available and is a way to showcase new resources as they are added.

I often hear teachers and principals lament about negative talk in the staff lounge. When we are in an upbeat, inspirational, and comfortable environment we are less likely to be negative and cynical. Creating a lounge that is bright, cheerful, and inviting is one positive step to thwarting less-than-productive conversations in the staff lounge.

Hallways

Hallways are some of the most traveled areas in any school. Don't underestimate the power they have in creating visual interest and learning opportunities. Many schools do an excellent job of filling their hallways with student work and visually attractive displays. Others neglect these areas and treat them as only practical areas for student movement. Encourage teachers to display student work by adding bulletin boards or cork stripping down the hallway.

One of my fifth-grade teachers used her area of the hallway to create a hall of presidents. Her students drew and researched each president. Their research report and drawings were displayed in chronological order in the hallway. Another time, this same teacher used her section of the hallway to recreate a visual representation of our Milky Way Solar System. The students paper-machéd and painted the planets to scale. These were hung from the ceiling using the entire hallway to recreate in scale the order from the sun and the distance of each planet from the sun. Research on the planets and other space facts were posted on the walls. This area became a learning environment for every student in the school. The hallway was on the second floor, but we had classes from the first floor taking trips upstairs to view and learn from these educational and student-made displays.

Use every inch of space you can. Attractively arrange tables and chairs in unused areas. I did this with some district furniture no one wanted. I picked out some old oak tables and chairs and during the slower winter months, a couple of workers from the maintenance crew refinished them. I placed them in stairwells and at the end of hallways. Teachers began to utilize them for small group work and meetings. Students could use the area to partner-read or have a nice desk area to complete unfinished work. This furniture also added a warmth and coziness to the stark hallways. I have seen many schools add table lamps, books, plants, beanbag chairs, and even rocking chairs to these areas, which would only enhance the visual appeal.

One of the easiest, cheapest, and quickest ways to brighten your hallways is to add colorful striping. With a few chalk lines and a couple of gallons of paint, you can add zip to your hallways instantly. Choose a couple of coordinating colors and paint a stripe down the hallway below it. Consider making one stripe wider than the other (i.e., first stripe 10 inches wide and second stripe 6 inches wide). If you are really adventurous, you can add peaks and zigzags to your design. Some schools have opted for bright geometric shapes painted throughout the hallways. These can create great visual interest in the school.

When I approached my custodian with the striping idea, he jumped right on the bandwagon. He was a huge help and got so excited by the project that he did most of the work himself. I know I was very lucky, but most parent organizations would volunteer to help and some staff members might, too. In fact, my parents were so thrilled with the hallway transformation, they volunteered to paint stripes in the cafeteria. It looked great!

The Cafeteria

This highly visible area should really give a sense of students and school to all who enter. Encourage student displays of work. At the secondary level, invite homerooms or departments to create exhibits of student projects or seasonal themed bulletin boards. These can become excellent advisory projects for individual homerooms. Have the school mascot and slogan painted on the wall. Decide upon a theme for the cafeteria and have a coordinated mural created. In the school that my children attend, the students voted to have a jungle theme in their cafeteria. Over the summer, parents volunteered to come in and create a jungle mural on the walls. The students were thrilled with the results, and felt empowered by the opportunity to cast their votes for their favorite theme.

I firmly believe that student (K–12) artwork is not displayed enough in the schools. The cafeteria can become an excellent place for everchanging exhibits of this wonderful work. Laminate black posterboard frames and frame the work to give it a more professional look. Change the artwork weekly or biweekly. Perhaps student council or office workers can make these changes when needed. Many schools have permanent student art displays, but changing exhibits provides the opportunity for constant sharing of many different pieces throughout the school year.

Many schools have permanent student art displays, but changing exhibits provides the opportunity for constant sharing of many different pieces throughout the school year.

Periodically provide table decorations. Whether they are seasonally themed or just a flower in a bud vase, this sets a more formal tone and students appreciate the added touch to their eating time. Some cafeterias have a "formal day" once a month. Tablecloths, flowers, and special napkins are used. Appropriate table manners are reviewed and students are to be on their best formal behavior this day. Many students are not aware of proper table manners, and this is an easy way to teach and reinforce this important societal skill at school.

Don't forget that most of these ideas are applicable to teacher eating areas as well. If the teachers in your building don't eat in the cafeteria with the students, then make sure that the place where they eat is comfortable and clean. Keep the room visually interesting and provide "creature comforts" whenever you can. Some formal touches can make teachers feel special. Tablecloths, centerpieces, and a bowl of mints or chocolates can add a little panache to your lunch setting. Providing nice paper napkins is always appreciated as is a special dessert periodically. Often your cooks will help you create these special treats, but you can also order sweets from a local bakery or deli. Some of you might even want to bake some goodies!

Conference Rooms

These are areas that deserve a bit of professional attention. Think about the events that occur in conference rooms (if you are lucky enough to even have one!): parent meetings, committee meetings, and community resource meetings, and they can also be a place to bring visitors for coffee and conversations. This room should be a location of which you and your staff can be proud to bring guests of the school into. Make this room attractive and pleasant. Framed artwork, comfortable seating, plants, paper and pencil for note taking, and a pitcher of water and glasses for refreshment are all items that can make this room comfortable for conferences and meetings.

Some schools also have a parent-teacher conference room. This room can be a bit less formal and house parent resources. A parent conference area can become a gathering place for visiting parents and a room where they can have parent board meetings or small committee meetings. This room can also be used for parent-teacher conferences or other special meetings between staff members and parents. Again, make this room welcoming with the same touches as above.

Inspirational parenting posters can adorn the walls and rocking chairs can fill the odd corners. A conference room of this type could also become a Parent Welcoming Center. When new families arrive, you could spend some time here with them getting acquainted. Have folders of basic school information prepared and add some school pencils, magnets, or notepads. Our student council made this a regular service project. They decorated the folders, placed the necessary materials inside, and presented the folder to the family upon arrival. Often they would give the new student a tour of the building while I was meeting with the parents. This was always a positive way to begin a new relationship with new families. Remember the basket of toys and books idea that was in the Classroom section? This is another good place to have a basket of goodies to keep young siblings playing contentedly.

Of course, one conference room can serve all purposes. The school where I was principal had a small room that housed a computer for management of a program unique to the school. This was all the room was used for. I immediately saw multiple uses for the space. I went to my PTA Board and shared my vision for this future conference room: a place for parent-teacher conferences, a resource center for parents to check out informational materials, a place for us to gather the visitors that came to our school, a place for teachers to have small group meetings when needed, and a location for meetings of groups of students for various school clubs. I asked for $150 to transform the room. They felt my idea had merit and gave me the money I asked for. I bought paint, wallpaper border, garage sale furniture, lamps, fabric for curtains, and a few parent resources to get our collection started. With the donation of the time and talents of some teachers and my custodian, we had ourselves a great little conference room. After the first year of using the conference room, the PTA was so impressed with its many functions they donated more money for additional resources.

Remember . . . It Can Begin with You

You can become the catalyst for change in your building. Start with one or two small projects and model your vision in your classroom. If you can generate some interest, then go for it! Visit other classrooms and other schools and invite your colleagues to go with you. As mentioned earlier, some schools have a climate committee devoted to continuously improving the look and tone of the school. One school shared that each spring and fall they have an all-school beautification day. Each classroom completes a project that will enhance the appearance of the school.

I have also mentioned several times in this chapter the involvement of custodians in this process. They can become key players in many of your classroom endeavors. Make sure they are treated with the same respect, dignity, and professionalism with which you treat your other peers. Their job can be just as demanding and difficult as anyone else's in the building. Let them know how much you appreciate them, and think of special ways to thank them for their efforts.

These changes can affect your personal morale, attitude, and energy in numerous positive ways. Creating an environment where you want to work and feel comfortable entering each day can only lead to greater productivity and job satisfaction. Happy teachers lead to happy students. Make your room feel like home . . . you deserve it!

Part IV

Peers and Cheers

and skill sets that we have ourselves. We can think back to high school when the prettiest girls often hung around their attractive peers. The best athletes tended to interactive with other "jocks." And, if we reflect back, unless we were with one of these "top tier" groups (whatever that means) we may not have felt comfortable interacting with them.

Though that may be high school, many times the same holds true as adults. Support staff members often feel most comfortable with others who are in similar roles. Teachers who also coach a sport may interact more with other faculty who do the same. Though this has some common sense, there may be another sorting and sifting taking place. It may have more to do with ability, skill, and effort than it does assignments. Many times in schools teachers tend to be most comfortable with others who are similar in their abilities. Often the best teachers interact with others who are also highly effective. The poorer teachers are often more connected to less-engaged peers and everyone else is somewhere in between. If you find yourself spending your informal time with teachers who are struggling in the classroom, who have challenges with student management, and who tend to be negative, it might be necessary to see if you are in the same pattern. By moving from this group and making attempts to connect with the most effective teachers, it can be easier to see how they approach teaching and their students.

It is very difficult to learn how to be great from average people. The reason they cannot teach you how to be outstanding is that they do not know how themselves. Think of learning from your peers and learning how to play tennis. Playing tennis with your best friend can be fun. However, if your friend is not more skilled than you are at the game, it is very difficult for your skill set to grow and be refined. And, if the friend has no skills at all, the only thing you spend your time doing is chasing around tennis balls that are spread all over the court (and maybe over the fence!). When our racquet opponent is at a higher level than us, we get much more practice and our improvement can occur much more rapidly. Now at times, it may bruise our

We learn best and fastest from others who know more than we do. It may cause us to move out of our traditional peer circle, but over time it helps us be much more effective in everything we do.

ego to play someone who overmatches our skill level, but gradually we can become more competitive at the game.

This same thing is true when learning from our peer teachers. When we observe someone who is more talented than we are or has a stronger work ethic, we may be intimidated or jealous, but we also have a chance to garner ideas that may benefit our classrooms and our students. Compare learning from other teachers with learning from a better tennis player and you will LOVE it. (Get it, LOVE it?) We learn best and fastest from others who know more than we do. It may cause us to move out of our traditional peer circle, but over time it helps us be much more effective in everything we do.

Peer Coaching

One avenue to begin focused instructional partnerships is through Peer Coaching. Peer Coaching has been defined and redefined over the years to meet the ever-changing needs of our teaching/learning environments in schools. An early definition of Peer Coaching relied heavily on the work of Costa and Garmston's Cognitive Coaching model. They defined Cognitive Coaching as this:

> a nonjudgmental process built around a planning conference, observation, and a reflecting conference. Anyone in the educational setting can become a cognitive coach—teachers, administrators, department chairs, or support personnel. A coaching relationship may be established between teacher and teacher, administrator and teacher, and/or administrator and fellow administrator. When a cognitive coaching relationship is established between two professionals with similar roles, or peers, it can be referred to as peer coaching. (Costa and Garmston, 2002)

This approach led to schools creating teams that would collaborate at the building and classroom levels. These teams would establish instructional goals that often coordinated with schoolwide goals. They created structures allowing colleagues to be in each other's rooms to observe lessons, conference at a later time, and provide positive feedback supporting their peers' work on instructional improvement.

Robbins (1991) defines Peer Coaching as a confidential process through which two or more professional colleagues work together to reflect on current practices; expand, refine, and build new skills; share ideas; teach one another; conduct classroom research; or solve problems in the workplace. Many teachers view Peer Coaching as a sort of dress rehearsal before opening night and as an opportunity to take risks and try new teaching approaches with someone they trust.

Although Peer Coaching seems to be the most prominent label for this type of activity, a variety of other names are used in schools: peer support, consulting colleagues, peer sharing and caring. Regardless of how coaching relationships are labeled, they all focus on the collaborative development, refinement, and sharing of craft knowledge. There are many powerful resources for coaching classroom instruction: Gudwin and Salazar-Wallace (2009), Kise and Russel (2010), and Marzano and Sims (2012).

It is important to note that Peer Coaching is never connected to the formal evaluation process used in the school setting. It is also not to be used for remediation of teachers. Most school systems see this as a venue to increase conversation about effective teaching, curriculum, and assessment. Principals love the Peer Coaching model because their primary job in this process is to simply create the opportunities for collaboration and then let the teachers learn from each other. They do not have to be in the conversation "loop," and this approach empowers their teachers to share and learn from each other without being monitored by administration. Most principals meet with Peer Coaching teams once or twice a year for informal updates on what they are learning and discovering through this cooperative experience. Valuable information is shared during these meetings, which can lead to schoolwide discussions or goal-setting based upon needs discovered through powerful Peer Coaching experiences.

Over the years Peer Coaching has involved formal and informal methods of implementation. Here is one form of a more formal approach to Peer Coaching that is being utilized in school settings:

Observations in Classrooms with Follow-Up Conferences—This approach involves peers coming into each other's classrooms to observe a lesson or portion of a lesson. The peer is only there as another set of eyes for the teacher being observed. Sometimes notes are taken or even a script of the lesson is done by the peer observer. These notes or scripts are left with the teacher being observed for private review. The two peers then meet for a Post-Conference follow-up to discuss talking points such as:

1. What was the lesson goal/objective?
2. What went well in the lesson?
3. What best practices or instructional strategies seemed to be effective?
4. What differentiation approaches were utilized?
5. What data collected would reflect student learning?
6. What would the teacher do differently next time?
7. What additional ideas would the teacher like to discuss?

This conference is private, and no notes are taken during the discussion. The teacher who was observed does the majority of the talking. The observer is free to share positive feedback and ask questions. Remember this must be nonjudgmental and must be simply the opportunity for comfortable flow of instructional dialogue.

After this is complete, the Peer Coaching partnership flips their roles. The first observer becomes the teacher being observed and the first teacher now gets to be the observer. After the lesson is taught, a follow-up conference is completed. Many Peer Coaching teams try to facilitate this process three to four times per year.

My first experience with Peer Coaching was during my time as a third-grade classroom teacher. My peer partner was the speech teacher in my building. This teacher was always pleasant and easy to work with, but taught outside the building in one of our trailers. I really had no clue what went on in her classroom. The Peer Coaching process allowed me into her instructional world, and I learned so much! Her observations in my classroom and our discussions led to her coming into my classroom once a week to facilitate vocabulary enrichment mini-lessons with my third graders. This would have never occurred had it not been for our Peer Coaching relationship.

Here are some less formal forms of collaboration that can lead to wonderful **Peer Connecting**.

Co-Planning and Teaching—Often Peer Coaching teams will co-plan a lesson or unit to meet district instructional objectives. This planning creates a collaborative and cooperative learning environment. Two heads are often better than one! The sharing of resources is imperative as we work to meet the diverse needs of the students in our classrooms. After the planning is complete, each teacher will instruct the lesson/unit that was co-planned. Daily conferences can keep each teacher focused and allow the opportunity to problem solve issues that arise together. It is also beneficial if observations can occur during this time to allow another venue for collaboration during this important teaching and learning.

Co-Teaching—This wonderful concept is gaining popularity and momentum as inclusion becomes the norm in many classrooms across the country. Co-teaching involves a partnership between professionals as they collaborate to improve the academic outcome for all students. These educators are placed in the same room and instruct a classroom of students in a unified and thoughtful fashion. There are several different approaches to co-teaching that involve both teachers maintaining an active role in the delivery of instruction in the classroom. The approaches range from one teacher instructing while one observes particular students and their needs, to actual team teaching where both teachers are delivering instruction together. This has been called "tag-team teaching" and can be complex to facilitate but very effective if done well. A recommended resource for co-teaching is *Collaboration Skills for School Professionals* (6th edition, 2010) written by Dr. Marilyn Friend and Dr. Lynne Cook.

Video Analysis—The demands of our busy school days sometimes do not easily facilitate us getting into each other's classrooms during the hours school is in session. You can still discuss instruction with your peers via watching video of each other delivering a lesson. A video camera can be set up in your classroom to capture your teaching, or some schools have student video teams who can film your teaching for you. If someone else records your teaching, make sure the equipment or recording is left with you. This is for your eyes only and for anyone you are willing to share it with. Personal reflection is first and foremost in this process. Invite your Peer Coaching partner to watch with you and have a discussion about the goals and learning that are processing in your classroom. If you have built a trusting relationship with your peer, this is a wonderful tool to grow and learn from.

"**Walk the School**"—Often when young children are learning to read and write, we encourage them to "Read the School." This involves the young learners taking a pointer with them and walking around the school hallways reading the environmental print on bulletin boards, posters, and signs. They point to words they know or recognize and read them.

I encourage each of you to "Walk the School" periodically. Notice bulletin boards, peek into classrooms (if you are not going to be a disruption), walk down the music hallway, cut through the gym, and talk to peers you see out and about. Try not to take this walk by yourself. Share this time with a colleague and discuss the teaching and learning you see in this building. Note things you like and tell those teachers you were impressed with what you saw or heard as you walked the school. There is a chance you saw something you wanted to learn more about. Follow up on this, and chances are that the teacher involved will be thrilled to share with you. This conversation could lead to some unique collaboration experiences while extending your instructional expertise. Another benefit to walking the school is the power of exercise and movement. Often you need a change of scenery and a different perspective. You can work on your healthy mind while also giving energy to a healthy body!

Book/Article Study Groups—When I was a principal, I tried to periodically have *Doughnuts and Discussion*. I would share an article with the staff and give them a few days to read the article. Then an invitation was sent out for a before-school discussion group meeting in which I provided doughnuts. This was never mandatory; it was just for those interested. We tried to make the meetings only last 15–20 minutes and I tried to choose articles that would lead to a very positive and productive discussion. I certainly did not want staff members to start their day on negative note! These discussions were relaxed and created connections among staff members who might not have regularly interacted (i.e., a P.E. teacher and a first-grade teacher). This could be done after school, too. *Treats and Talk* might be a good name for it, and popcorn or some popular munchie snack could be provided.

You certainly don't have to be the principal to facilitate this in your building. Make sure you have the administrator's blessing and run past him or her the article you will be using. If people know what is going to be discussed, are aware that food is provided, and have assurance the gathering will be short, I promise you will get takers! Once others hear about this positive and fun "meeting," you can be assured your attendance will grow.

The same can be done with a book, discussing one chapter at a time. In fact, this book has been used for that exact purpose! The important factors to remember are to choose quality reading material, provide food if you can, and make sure the meetings have beginning and ending times that are realistic for the busy teacher's life.

Instructional Rounds—Many principals do regular informal visits to classrooms. And, if they don't, they should. There are lots of reasons for this, including the chance to reinforce and guide instructional practices and reduce the likelihood of more formal evaluation visits being seen as "events." Because of this, most teachers have become familiar with and used to other adults in their classrooms. One benefit for principals is that they are able to increase their personal knowledge of effective teaching, which they can then use to facilitate these practices throughout the school. However, rather than waiting for the principal to be the middleman (or lady), you should get the benefits of these other staff members by initiating this practice yourself.

Some teachers choose to join the principal on his or her instructional rounds or walk-throughs so that they can gain ideas from peers. But there is no need to wait for this; see if you can get this practice started on your own. Take fifteen or twenty minutes a week and visit several other classrooms. By doing this, you will quickly have the opportunity to add to your teaching repertoire. You will gain ideas on the best ways to start instruction, on questioning techniques, etc., and it is much easier to "borrow" these approaches from someone else than to think of them yourself. So, put on your walking shoes and take advantage of the outstanding colleagues in your school!

In closing this chapter, I would like to share an experience I had. I had the pleasure of training two high schools to utilize a Peer Coaching model. At the completion of three years, I asked them to write personal definitions of Peer Coaching. Here are a few:

> "Peer Coaching is a means through which teachers can reflect on education practices and talk constructively about the profession."

> "Working together to enhance the learning environment of all students. All teachers can benefit from a system that allows for the positive exchange of ideas while working toward a common goal."

> "The development of professional friendships. The appreciation of learning and teaching styles among colleagues. A helping hand . . . an encouraging word . . . a peer to turn to."

> "Peer Coaching is observing and becoming inspired by what one sees. It is talking and sharing with colleagues as a means of growth and improvement."

As you move forward to find positive peer connections, be acutely aware of peer pressure vs. peer power. Peer pressure can keep us from improving and drag us down negative paths that lead to unhappiness and loss of passion for teaching. Peer power enables us to do things beyond what we might be able to do on our own. Peer power can liven us up and move us forward in ways we could not dream of in isolation. Find ways to collaborate and celebrate the power of your peers.

14

The Teaching World Is a Twitter

> **❝** *Teamwork is the fuel that allows* **❞**
> *common people to attain uncommon results.*
>
> —*Andrew Carnegie*

Some of the most valuable teaching advice and ideas I have received in my career have been from my peers and colleagues. Not too long ago, the only peers you interacted with regularly were the ones in your own schools and buildings. In the last chapter we talked about how to learn from and make connections from those in your own school. Historically, we used to think of teachers as a bunch of independent contractors who share a common parking lot, but hopefully we have moved past that in our own schools. Fellow teachers can be a tremendous resource. However, what if you are the only teacher of a certain subject in your school? What happens if you are the youngest staff member, the only newbie, or have questions that you would not feel comfortable asking those in your immediate physical vicinity?

Periodically, you might have attended conferences (if the budget allowed) to meet new colleagues, or you might have taken a college course that created the opportunity to gain new insights from other educators. Journals, books, and videos helped to round out the opportunities to learn the newest and best innovations in education. These are all still valuable options, but there are many ways to go above and beyond these limitations. My, how times have changed . . .

Twitter

I absolutely am *absolutely sold* on Twitter. I cannot believe I even just wrote that last sentence! If you would have told me two years ago that interacting with educators all over the world in 140 characters or fewer would have me feeling professionally fulfilled, I would have told you that you must have me confused with someone else. How could this thing called Twitter expand my knowledge and allow me to stay current with all things education? Two years ago, I thought Twitter was just a silly invention that allowed movie stars and professional sports royalty to let the whole world know where they ate their lunch that day and who they partied with last night. Last summer, my husband shared an article with me about a new innovation in reading assessment. I loved the article and asked him where he got it. His reply, "Pulled it from a tweet." Seriously??!! It just sounded so ridiculous. Then he began to show me his "timeline," all of the reputable and interesting people he "followed," and some of the valuable links embedded into "tweets." I was amazed and intrigued. From that moment on, I could not get enough Twitter. I set up my account and slowly "lurked and learned" as I began following people and organizations I had respected for years. I also found new education innovators who were sharing amazing strategies, knowledge, and expertise. Little did I know, but I was developing my own Personal Learning Network via a social media outlet I had once deemed a humorous waste of time. I had embarked on the professional journey of a lifetime.

Twitter is not an obligation. E-mail is an obligation. Facebook is an obligation. With e-mail, I am scared to check mine if I walk out of a two-hour meeting. Every e-mail I receive I must respond to, delete, or save until later. What a pain. The only e-mail I ever am excited about is the one from the Romanian princess telling me I just won three million rubles. Other than that they are all burdens. Even Facebook is an obligation. I hate to even open it because I am scared whose birthday it might be today. I hope it is not the high school classmate whom I never really liked. Not that I am obligated to give them fake birthday greetings. I guess my only choice is to try to friend more people whose birthday is February 29th so that I am limited to having to interact with them once every four years. But Twitter is different!

Social Media

I would be remiss if I did not discuss the overall power of social media in this day and age. I must admit that I avoided the Myspace trend, and I have not gotten too deeply into Facebook. I know it allows so many social connections to occur and has been highly popular. Trust me, I have taken a lot of flack from friends and relatives over the years about this decision.

But I chose the profession of education. I love my profession and know that I must consistently be a positive role model for my future, current, and past students. In addition, I really don't want portions of my life out there for the masses to see. Not that I have anything to hide, but educators need to be cautious about how much information shared is too much information.

I do know that many educators use Facebook as a professional interactive tool with their students, parents, and families and do amazing things with it. I would suggest maintaining an open mind about its use, but like with any social media site, be cautious about how much you share and the appropriateness of your content. Once it is out there . . . it is out there.

A social media tool that has hooked me is Pinterest. This wonderful site allows you to customize and "pin" items into personal categories you determine based on your interests. My daughter in college showed me this one summer and I was intrigued. My first categories were decorating, recipes, and holidays. Soon I realized there was a world of information on Pinterest that focused on education. Naturally, I now have categories (or "boards" as they are called in Pinterest land) relating to teaching, reading instruction, classroom management, and classroom organization. The options are endless, and you can create your own Pinterest world that feeds into your personal interests. For me, I see a distinct difference in how I use Pinterest and Twitter. Twitter is my current, up-to-date connection with the world. I check Twitter in three to four minutes and catch up. I find myself spending a great deal of time on Pinterest when I log in. I can really get pulled in and lose track of time (in a good way). I use both mediums to gain expertise and knowledge, but utilize them in different ways in my day-to-day life.

> *Twitter is my current, up-to-date connection with the world. I check Twitter in three to four minutes and catch up.*

Now, back to Twitter. As I stated earlier, I feel that my experience with Twitter has been a powerful professional journey for me. I feel like I am getting the national, state, and regional pulse on education daily. I follow the U.S. Secretary of Education, our State Secretary of Education, reputable media outlets with specific education Twitter feeds, and respected, high-profile organizations. These resources keep me connected with the most real-time current events in education. In the past, I would wait to read this information in the paper, in a professional journal, or in an e-mail. I now have multiple outlets to keep abreast of important education news that can impact my chosen profession.

I also follow like-minded educators who expand my knowledge base and push my critical thinking about best practices in education. These individuals have reenergized my love of learning and have given me a world of ideas that have improved my teaching and pedagogy. I share these wonderful ideas with my college students and expand their collections of teaching and learning tools. I am truly amazed at the limitless ideas that are shared each and every day. The group of people I follow has become my Personal Learning Network (PLN). The joy of having a PLN is that you can customize it to meet your individual needs. I am a teacher of reading and language arts courses at the collegiate level. I have sought out and follow those individuals and organizations whom I respect and whom I know tweet only ideas and practices of the highest degree of integrity and effectiveness. Because of the quality of my PLN, opening my Twitter each day is consistently exciting and enriching.

Over the years, I have lectured my students about Facebook and other social media, warning them that as educators, they must be very, very careful about what they post. One misstep could cost them their chance of getting a job and even holding on to a job they have procured. I found myself tired of this lecture and have embraced Twitter as a method for me to model to my students how to use social media in a productive and professional way. I encourage them to be part of the chats that take place on Twitter. One of the hour-long weekly chats is created solely for new teachers (#ntchat). Every Wednesday from 8 p.m. to 9 p.m. Eastern time they can connect with new teachers all over the world and discuss their most pressing issues and concerns. This chat is moderated by experienced educators who can guide and support new teachers in their first years of teaching. This connection with my college students has been exhilarating for me and allowed us to collaborate beyond the classroom forever. I can still support them in their first years of teaching when they feel alone, and I have taught them how to create a PLN that can nurture their professional growth as they embark into the wonderful world of teaching.

In addition to new teacher chats (#ntchat), there are also social studies chats (#soschat), kindergarten chats (#kinderchat), math chats (#mathchat), leadership chats (#satchat), special education chats (#spedchat), etc. The site at *www.cybraryman.com/edhashtags.html* has a continually updated list of all of the options for educators to interact with their peers on Twitter. Whatever area you are in, you have the opportunity to regularly interact with and learn from some of the brightest minds in your chosen field. There are even several general education chats each week on various topics (#edchat).

Many educators have embraced Twitter, but others are wary and cannot see it as a useful tool. The only way to convince people is through their own experience. I always encourage people to open a Twitter account (it is very simple and you don't even have to use your real name if you don't want to). Search for people and organizations you respect. Follow them and see who they follow (this is easily done if their account is not locked). Then I encourage people to "Lurk and Learn." This is a Twitter phrase that just means to read and watch your Twitter feed. Don't feel the need to begin to tweet immediately. Get comfortable with the setup and add to your "follow" list as you locate interesting and knowledgeable organizations and people to follow. I cannot overly stress the importance of making sure you follow quality educators and organizations you admire and trust. This kind of follow-list will give you the very best, accurate, and inspiring information in your daily Twitter timeline.

If you are already using some form of technology tool (blogs, wikis, Twitter, Facebook, Pinterest, etc.) to enhance your professional journey, congrats and continue! If you have not embraced social media yet, I truly hope you will give serious consideration to at least trying it. The Internet will allow you to easily research your options. Try one, start small, and don't get discouraged if everything doesn't go smoothly at first. Stay determined, and I promise you will reap rewards beyond your wildest dreams!

Whatever Is Next

We were very hesitant to write this chapter. We knew that by the time the book was out, Twitter, Facebook, Pintrest, etc. could already be yesterday's news. However, rather than exclude these sites, we chose to include them because our purpose was to emphasize the importance and the ability to connect with peers from around the world. In the previous chapter, we talked about the importance of learning from the best—playing tennis with a better opponent. Unfortunately, at times, the atmosphere, tone, or culture in our own school is not as conducive to sharing as it should be. Teachers who are creative and innovative may not be viewed in a very positive light by their peers in the same building. Though this statement is very sad, it is also too often true. Feeling alone is not fun. Social media—whatever its current form is—is a powerful way to connect with others who have similar talents and philosophies no matter where they are located.

The United States is continually compared to other countries. Depending on the current news we are anywhere from 10th to 30th in the world in education—whatever that means. In the past, when we would hear of the success in another country—one of the latest "hot spots" is Finland—we would have to just put our heads down and be jealous. However, now, with Twitter and other forms of social media, we don't have to lament our fate; we can affect it. Instead of reading about what some teachers are doing in another state or part of the world, interact and learn from them! When we think about peers who are on the cutting edge, usually it is the best and the brightest who have the confidence to take that leap. Well, these are the same colleagues who we want to learn from. And there is another reason you need to be a part of whatever the current journey is. Other people deserve to have a chance to learn from the best and sometimes that best person is you!

Social media—whatever its current form is—is a powerful way to connect with others who have similar talents and philosophies no matter where they are located.

Climb aboard and strap in! We don't know what the latest ride is, but we bet it is a good one!

15

Working with Negative People

> **"** *An incompetent teacher is much worse than an incompetent surgeon, because an incompetent surgeon can only cut up one person at a time.* **"**

One of the biggest challenges we face in keeping up our own positive morale is the struggle and impact that our most negative coworkers, peers, and others have on us and on the entire organization. There are several ways in which their impact is detrimental. However, the aspect we have the most control over is how much power we choose to give them. We give away too much power to these negative people. And it isn't just us. Everyone in our organization does. Even as peers we give away too much power to our most negative coworkers. People in leadership roles often make decisions based on the least effective staff members rather than the most effective and important ones. Let's take a look at some examples. We will start with an understanding of how we give away too much power to our peers and then follow up with examples of how, when we are in leadership roles, we can give away too much power to the most negative people in a group.

Giving Power Away to Negative Peers

One of the faults that we have in education is that we give way too much power to our most difficult peers and other negative people in our organization. This needs to stop. It is important that we consistently remind ourselves that the essential people on a faculty are the positive and productive people. Too often decisions are based on the least important and productive people in a group. Let us look at an example.

A few years ago I was doing a weeklong workshop in the summer for a school. This school had 45 faculty members. Forty-two of these dedicated educators had voluntarily given up a week of their summer to attend my workshop. Whenever there is a substantial length of time to work with a staff, I try to start out the week with an hour or so of very positive, fun, engaging activities. We got off to a great and productive start, which I felt had set the tone in a favorable manner for the week. When we took our first break, one of the teachers from the school approached me. She commented that the first part of the day had gone very well and she was looking forward to the rest of the week. However, she added, the people who needed to be there were not there. Then she asked me what should be done. I told her I appreciated her question and asked if she would be kind enough to ask it in front of the entire group once the break was over.

Once everyone returned she raised her hand and said, "We were talking at break that we think this will be a valuable week, but we also feel that the teachers who need to be here are not here. What do you think we should do?"

It is important that we consistently remind ourselves that the essential people on a faculty are the positive and productive people.

I paused, looked each person in the eye, and said, "I can tell you what I would do. I would praise the Lord. Ask yourself if those missing people walked into the room right now, would that make your week better or worse? Would you wave them over to sit by you? Of course not. You would hope they would sit as far away as possible. And so would the other people in here. So let's make sure we do not let these people, who are not even here, ruin our week."

The real issue was to examine the amount of power we were going to give to our most negative staff peers. We were going to let them ruin our fun week and they were not even there! That is power and we must stop relinquishing it. We must also help everyone we work with stop giving power to our most negative coworkers.

Additionally, when I do workshops for schools, one of the questions those in attendance will ask is, "How do we get those people who were absent 'caught up'?" My first response is to ask if they are positive and productive peers. If they are, then we develop strategies to bring them up to speed. However, if they are negative and just skipped the meeting or workshop for no good reason, then I say don't do anything to catch them up. This isn't to be mean. Quite the opposite. If you have a weeklong workshop that you miss and someone can "catch you up" in twenty minutes, then you are glad you missed the workshop! Instead, if you feel like you really missed something of value, then you will make it a special point to be in attendance the next time.

The Role of the Leader

Leaders often make decisions based on their most negative and resistant people in a group or organization. That is human nature. We are often worried about how the most cynical staff member will react or how the few "gripers" will talk about us in the lounge. Being aware of their potential reactions is fine. Maybe it is even wise. However, making decisions with them in mind rather than the most positive and productive people in mind is a big mistake. It is a common occurrence, way too common, but one that must stop immediately.

When deciding whether or not to implement a new policy or "rule" there is a quick three-question quiz to determine whether this policy is likely to have a positive or a negative effect on morale. Here are the three questions:

1. What is the true purpose in implementing this rule or policy?

2. Will it actually accomplish the purpose?
3. How will the most positive and productive people in the group feel about it?

This sounds very basic, and it is; however, it can be a powerful measure of not only future implementations, but also can help determine the value of current procedures. Let us apply these questions to a scenario that is very common in many schools.

An issue many schools face is exceeding the copy machine budget. In many educational settings, in about mid-February, it is realized that the copier budget for the entire year is almost gone. It is also realized that often there are a couple of people who are constantly at the copier and may seem to be using it in a very disproportionate manner compared to both the other faculty, and maybe even to their own effectiveness. Well, one thing that happens in many organizations is a sign gets posted by the copy machine. Often the sign looks something like this:

Limit 20 Copies!

With this scenario in mind we can apply these same three questions to rules and procedures we attempt to implement in order to control difficult staff members and determine whether they are likely to have an appropriate and positive effect on a school.

Other common scenarios that arise in schools are faculty using supplies (folders, Post-it notes, paper, etc.) at a rate that will exceed the budget. Most likely there are just a few people who are using things in an inappropriate manner or maybe even using some of these items for personal uses. As a result there is a temptation to implement much tighter restrictions on using the copier or accessing supplies. It may be required that all staff sign a piece of paper indicating how many copies they make. Or there might be a requirement to have all staff sign up on a list when they take any supplies. There could even be a memo issued expecting staff to reduce their usage of copies or supplies—kind of a guilty-until-proven-innocent approach. We can apply our three rules and determine if these approaches are appropriate and effective.

1. **What is the true purpose in implementing this rule or policy?**

   Your first reaction might be to say that the purpose is to tick people off. However, that is the result, not the purpose. The purpose in putting forth this rule is to prevent those who are wastefully using the copier or taking too many supplies from continuing these practices. In other words, it is to stop those who are abusing the copier from doing so.

2. **Will it actually accomplish the purpose?**

   If people are making inappropriate use of the copier they most likely know it is inappropriate and they just choose to do what they want. No one is under the assumption that it is okay to run copies of their Christmas card letter on the school copier. Is this likely to prevent the inappropriate usage of materials? Probably not. Though even if your answer is maybe or yes (that it will accomplish the purpose of getting them to stop abusing the copier), we still need to examine the potential result to the vast majority—the most important staff members—those who already follow these standards or rules before they are even implemented. Thus we will attempt to answer the third question, which is often the most important.

3. **How will the most positive and productive people feel about this policy?**

   High achievers, which includes the most effective teachers, are often very guilt-driven. They are likely to assume that any time a new rule or procedure is implemented it could be because they have done something wrong. When it is shared with the staff that the copier is being used excessively, the high achievers think to themselves about that time three years ago when they ran 25 copies for an activity when they ended up only needing 22. They are the most likely faculty members to restrict their usage of materials or supplies. Is this going to have a productive effect on others in the school?

As teachers, sometimes we do the same thing to students. Two common examples are punishing all students because a few were uncooperative, or implementing more complex procedures because one person abused your flexible nature. But, if you ask yourself these three questions, you will make your students and yourselves much happier and have more productive results.

Let's Get Out in Those Hallways!

I would like to present one more example that might help clarify the importance of making every decision based on the most positive and productive people. If we think how we feel when this happens to us, it can help us be more sensitive when we lead a group or committee.

Take an example of a large, traditional high school. Typical of a school like this is that the day is composed of seven classes of around fifty minutes each. Another part of that day is something commonly referred to as "passing time." This is the five minutes or so when no one knows who is in charge of the school and the students seem to be in a mass state of excitement and hysteria. If you as an adult are caught in this, you feel sort of like a salmon swimming upstream.

What is our guess that principals would like their teachers to be doing during this time? We would imagine that most principals would prefer to have their teachers out in the hallways monitoring the students during the passing time. And, typically, for the first week or so of school, many teachers are out by their doors monitoring the hallways. But then, we all get busy, time is of the essence, and we become less and less likely to be out in the halls. Besides, since fewer of our peers are out in the hallways, why should we be out there?

Well, then February rolls along and the principal, who like all of the teachers is a little tired at this point of the year, becomes frustrated that more of the teachers are not out in the hallways. So, the principal issues a reminder—the all-powerful memo. Well, of course, we can all imagine the reaction. Teachers pull the memo out of their mailboxes and immediately salute the piece of paper it is on and think to themselves, "Yes sir (or m'am), just let me know the time, the place, and the duty, and I'll be there." I guess this is not really what happens, is it?

Anyhow, let's take a look at what happened here. The principal issued a memo based on the least effective teachers, not those who were actually out in the hallways. Is there any way that this could be handled differently?

Let's take a look at two possible scenarios and we will use a faculty meeting, instead of a memo. Remember the purpose—to get more teachers out in the hallway. Why wouldn't the purpose be to get every teacher out in the hallway? Because if the expectation is based on perfection then any one person can ruin it for us. And we are not going to let our negative people do that any longer. Additionally, we are going to divide the faculty into two groups. Superstars on one side and mediocres on the other, keeping in mind that our superstars are already the most likely to be out in the hallway.

Scenario One

We join the faculty meeting already in progress, and the principal is speaking:

"Hey, folks, listen. I expect every one of you to be out in the hallway between classes. Today there were two fights in that hallway and there were no teachers out there. I expect every one of you to be out there between each class. We talked about that at the first meeting of the year and it is even in the faculty handbook!"

Unfortunately, approaches like this are way too common. Let's use our three rules and examine the results.

Question 1: What Was the Purpose?
Well, the purpose was to get more people out in the hallway. How do the superstars feel? Most likely—TICKED OFF!

"What are you talking to me for?" they often think. "Why don't you talk to them!"

Question 2: Will It Actually Accomplish the Purpose?

Are the superstars more likely or less likely to be out in the hallway tomorrow? Less likely. And, in addition, if they are out there they are likely to be in a bad mood, because of the approach we used.

However, wasn't it the mediocres we were really talking to? Let's examine how they feel—at least those who were even AT the meeting. What is amazing is that they could not care less. As a matter of fact, most of them were not even paying attention. And, those who were will think, "If I was going to get yelled at, I am glad I wasn't out there!"

Question 3: How Will the Most Positive and Productive People Feel About It?

Unfortunately, the best people will have a less positive view of the leader. Additionally, the mediocres will usually feel worse also, or at best the same about the person in charge. Even the group it was focused on had no productive impact.

Scenario Two

We join the faculty meeting already in progress, and the principal is speaking:

"Hey, folks, listen. I know how full everyone's plates are and I just appreciate, so much, those of you who have made that extra effort to be out in the hallway. Today I happened to be out in the hallway and there were two boys who were about to fight. There was also a teacher out in that hall, and I don't even think the teacher saw those boys. Anyhow, right before they came to blows, one of the boys saw the teacher, tapped his potential combatant on the shoulder, and pointed to the teacher. They both shrugged and walked off in separate directions. I just appreciate so much those of you who are out in the hallway between classes. It makes our school a safer place for all of our students, and it makes our school a safer place for all of us. Thank you."

Let's revisit our three rules and examine the results.

Question 1: What Was the Purpose?

The purpose was to get more people out in the hallway. How do the superstars feel? PRETTY DARN GOOD!

Question 2: Will It Actually Accomplish the Purpose?

Amazingly, most of the superstars probably think that the principal was talking about them since they didn't see any students about to fight! And, they are more likely to be out in the hall tomorrow, and, probably even the days after that.

But, how do the mediocres feel? Some probably feel a little guilty. Some still were not paying attention. And, some could not care less. But, are they more likely or less likely to be out in the hall tomorrow? They will not all be out there, of course, but at least for some of them, they are more likely.

Question 3: How Will the Most Positive and Productive People Feel About It?

Fortunately, the best people will have a more positive view of the leader and the school. They enjoyed the praise without being singled out. This is called anonymous public praise. Those who were doing what was right think the leader was talking about them. Amazingly, even if no one was out in the hall, this approach still works. Because, if no one was out there, then no one could know that no one else was out there!

Additionally, the mediocres will usually feel better, or the same about the leader. Some will want to get a piece of that praise, so they will venture out in the hall the next day. Often, even the most resistant people will go out into the hall at least one day—even if it is only to see who the goody two-shoes are who are out in the hall!

What's in It for Me?

The benefits to the group are pretty obvious. People will feel better and more valued. However you may be asking, how does this make me feel better? Think about the time with a group of students when you were least proud of your behavior. Maybe you lost your cool, yelled, or laced your verbal barrage with sarcasm. How did you feel? Of course, we regretted that we chose to behave in that fashion and it may have even been a challenge to look those students in the eye for a while—at least, until we apologized. Now, think about which type of student caused us to feel most ashamed to be seen this way. Most likely it is the student we had the most respect and regard for.

What is in it for us is that we can feel better about the way we treat others. The more respect and dignity we show for others, the more respect and dignity we feel for ourselves.

It Is Up to You

We are all aware that we choose how to behave every day. The decisions we make include how we are going to act and how we will choose to treat others. Making sure that we take control of ourselves is an essential step to reducing the impact and influence we have on negative people that we come in contact with. After all, controlling difficult people first requires that we control ourselves.

16

Make Your Teaching SPARKLE!

❝_When teachers reflect on their
careers, they will be proudest of the_ **❞**
moments when they taught with love.

In this era of high-stakes testing and accountability, I have observed basic education curriculum used in classrooms start to make some shifts. This curriculum has become very scripted for teachers, and the flexibility that teachers once felt to use their intuitive professional judgment has somewhat diminished. Please know that I applaud a standards-driven, outcomes-based curriculum. This instructional focus has helped teachers know exactly what should be taught.

When the standards-based movement began, teachers were given the professional latitude to decide how to teach these standards based upon the needs of their students. Since the passage of the No Child Left Behind federal legislation, I have watched this latitude diminish. Only "approved" curriculum can be used, assessments must be given with increased regularity, and deviation from scope and sequence, even slightly, is frowned upon in many school districts. Some of this has left teachers feeling that being spontaneous and facilitating teachable moments are really not regular options for them. The curriculum timelines are tight and district rules are rules.

As I have journeyed with my college students into schools, I have seen this written on teachers' faces and evidenced in their practice. When my students assume teaching roles in these classrooms, they must follow the district guidelines, and we accept this. But we have decided to add a little "something" to our lessons. We wanted this something to spice things up and get the students really excited and engaged in their learning. We knew that it couldn't take much time and needed to complement the instructional objectives in each classroom. With this goal in mind, we developed what we call "Sparkle." We even have developed an acronym for our approach to SPARKLE:

SPARKLE

    S – Sharing

    P – Powerful

    A – Activities

    R – Really

    K – Keeps

    L – Learners

    E – Engaged

Sharing powerful activities really keeps learners engaged! Isn't this the truth? The belief is that creating a special moment or moments in each lesson will help the learners engage and *really* remember the content being presented.

Richards (2011) calls these moments tiny shots of FUN or "Fun Sparkles." Our students are required to have a "Sparkle" element in each reading lesson they teach. This part of the lesson can be as simple as a quick video clip or a personal anecdote that is shared with the class. We suggest making it something different, thoughtful, exciting, and tailored to your students' needs. Here are a few examples you might try:

1. Use a visual aid to make the objective "come to life."
2. Find a video clip to illustrate content.
3. Create a riddle or puzzle to introduce the concept.
4. Share a personal story that connects the learners to your lesson.
5. Find an interactive website that would allow the class to play a game or complete an activity to complement the content.
6. Invite a guest speaker or mystery guest—this could be an actual guest who has expertise to share or you dressed up using props, hats, wigs, etc. to introduce an important historical figure or story character.
7. Use technology to connect to other classes, schools, or countries that are appropriate to your focus.
8. Facilitate extension activities. These may take a bit longer, but will take the children's mastery of concepts to higher levels. Here are a some extension activities:
   a. Create a timeline to chronicle a story or historic event.
   b. Make a poster to advertise an event or character from your content.
   c. Write a poem about a character or event.
   d. Draw a diagram that illustrates a math or science concept.
   e. Design a travel brochure for the area you are studying in geography or social studies.
   f. Write a song about the content of the lesson.
   g. Draw a picture of a gift you might give a character or important person you are studying.
   h. Write a letter to a historical figure or author.

Another wonderful way to spice up any lesson is through the use of sticky notes. For years, I have been amazed at the versatility of these sticky little pieces of paper and wish I had invented them! As a classroom teacher and college professor, I LOVE to weave these into a lesson to engage thinking and facilitate personal connections to content.

Here are some of the ways I have used sticky notes and have seen them used in classrooms:

♦ If you have a "morning meeting" or gathering time each day, let students write their contribution on a sticky note and place it on a special board in your classroom. Train them to do this when they first enter your room each day. This allows you to look through them, find the most pressing/important ones for the day, and address them in your meeting time. This removes the need for raising hands as they vie for your attention. Tell students if you don't get to theirs and it is very important, they can tell you privately later.

♦ When you introduce a difficult or complex concept, have a quadrant with levels of understanding and have students place a Post-it note as they leave class that day in the spot they feel like their comprehension level is. Then prior to your next class or the next day, you can have a chance to reflect where learning is. At the secondary level, you could even compare each of your classes to see if you may have differed in your approach to see which one had the higher level of grasping the concept.

♦ Give each student one sticky note. Have him or her identify a favorite part of a story or reading selection and be prepared to tell the class why it was his or her favorite.

♦ Let students place sticky notes on vocabulary words that "sparkled" or made the story/text more interesting to them. Discuss these as a class or in small groups.

♦ Summarize reading material on a sticky note and place it in the margin for future reference.

♦ Use sticky notes to create on writing storyboards. These can be easily moved around to adjust content and flow.

♦ Peer feedback on writing assignments can be made on sticky notes. This way students are not writing on another student's work. I have personally seen that this kind of feedback option is more comfortable for students to use.

- What Stuck With You Today? Have each student write something he or she will remember from the lesson, and have a bulletin board or another place in the classroom where students can post their responses. This gives you valuable formative feedback on your lesson and solidifies their learning. This is a great exit slip idea for middle/high school.

- Sticky notes are also great for collecting questions. Often our time is limited in class, so questions don't get answered. Have students keep running lists on sticky notes and give them to you at the end of class. If a question gets answered during class, they can just cross it off before they turn their lists in to you. This feedback allows you to understand critical points of misunderstanding and address specific student issues later or in your next class session.

- The fact that sticky notes come in different colors is also useful. If you are teaching sentence structure/parts, you could use one color for the verbs, one color for nouns, etc. If you are teaching a particular part of sentence structure (e.g., direct objects), the color could be just for that particular part of the sentence. Making and breaking words into sentences becomes enjoyable for students as they "move" the parts during instruction.

The 3M Post-it website (*http://teachers.post-it.com/wps/portal/3M/en_US/Post-it-Teachers/Home/*) offers hundreds of teaching ideas divided by subject area, grade levels, and teaching techniques. These ideas were submitted by practicing teachers and are collected here in one location for ease of reference.

This concept of making your lessons "Sparkle" is simple. What you do does not have to be time-consuming, just engaging. No matter what your grade level, subject, or area, having a more dynamic and exciting instructional approach can help recharge the batteries of our students and ourselves. We are never too old to get a gold star, smiley face, or attaboy, and neither are our students.

We are never too old to get a gold star, smiley face, or attaboy, and neither are our students.

Challenge yourself to look at each lesson before you teach it and ask yourself if it includes something interesting and attention-getting. If it appears boring and lackluster to you, then you can bet it will appear that way to your students. Put in a little extra effort to make learning enjoyable and meaningful for your students. Utilizing and integrating technology is a wonderful way to provide that "oomph" that your instruction may have been missing. That little extra "punch" to your teaching will also energize you. Sparkle on!

17

Students—The Most Precious Commodity

> **"** *Teaching kids to count is fine,*
> *but teaching them what counts is best.* **"**
>
> —*Bob Talbert*

We have discussed many ideas throughout this book that involve taking care of yourself. Many of the ideas have involved things you can do with your students that also will assist you. Let's take a look at a couple of other approaches that can help you and the valued students you come in contact with. Understanding these relationships more thoroughly may allow you to be more effective as an educator.

The "They Feel Good— You Feel Good" Cycle

One of the most basic ways to make your job enjoyable is to make the environment for those around you more positive. If everyone around us approaches each day in a more positive light, then often it can help bring us up when we feel less enthusiastic. Students will approach their classrooms each day in a manner that is most dependent on how they and their peers are treated in that class on a regular basis. If they are treated with respect and dignity, that will be the frame of mind with which they approach the room. If they are interacted with in a less appropriate manner, then this is how they will walk into the class or school.

It is essential that we are well aware of our role as educators in the mind-set of students. Think of an elementary or secondary school you know. Ask yourself this question: "Would you bet that you could guess which teacher in that school will send the most students to the office NEXT year?" Most teachers and principals would take this bet and even give odds. And this is without even knowing which students that teacher will have!

We determine the approach and attitudes that our students will have. We cultivate the dispositions of those in our classrooms and schools.

You might be thinking that you all must be psychic. However, it is really pretty easy. The variable is not the students; the variable, of course, is the teacher. We determine the approach and attitudes that our students will have. We cultivate the dispositions of those in our classrooms and schools. This is a powerful responsibility, but it is also a wonderful opportunity. Being aware of this and working to build these kind of relationships can go a long way toward your feeling valued at work.

One way to approach this is to treat all students like you would treat your best students. It reminds me of the idea of treating students (and everyone) with an "As If" rather than an "As Is" attitude. I'd like to share with you my first experience with this belief.

Treat All Students "As If" They Were Your Best Students

A friend makes his living buying apartments, fixing them up, and renting them out. He has been tremendously successful and has accumulated great wealth doing this. He started out with little or no money and has become quite an entrepreneur in this field. One night we were discussing his success, and I asked him this question: "What do you do if you buy an apartment building and there are tenants living there that you do not want in your building? How do you handle it, especially if they have a long-term lease?"

His reply was surprising, yet offered great insight to how we should work with others. He said, "I have learned that if I buy an apartment building and I fix it up, the tenants who I originally were hesitant about do one of two things. They either move out or, more likely, they start acting like they deserve to live there."

I understood what he meant by this. A few people who get treated with respect and dignity may become so uncomfortable that they withdraw from the situation. However, the vast majority start acting with respect and dignity. It is true with students also.

Let's say you are walking down the hallway of your school and all of the students are supposed to be in class. However, heading in your direction are the two biggest "troublemakers" in the school. What do you say to them? Traditionally it is things like, "Where are you supposed to be?" or "Whose class are you out of?" Often your tone is very accusatory.

Contrast this with a typical approach if the future valedictorian and salutatorian are walking down the hall when everyone else is in class. Often our response would be something like, "Hi. How are you doing?" or possibly, "Have a nice day!" Quite a difference, isn't there? We sure did not treat all the students "as if" they were good, did we? Instead, what we need to do is determine an approach that will assist us in both situations.

Treating everyone— students and adults alike— as if they want to do what is right will make them more likely to do what is right and will help them view us in a much more positive light.

When we see students in either setting we could say something like, "Hi. Can I help you?" Amazingly, the two high-achieving students will see that as a positive. By the same token, the two students that may have heightened our suspicions will not see it in a negative light, either. And, it will help us get as much information as the more negative and accusatory approaches.

It is very similar to being a clerk in a store. If I approach potential shoplifters in a negative tone, they will not admit what their intentions are. Instead, they might even have more of an incentive to seek revenge. Even worse, if they were not there to shoplift, then I have potentially lost a customer. And, incredibly, as a store manager, if I approach enough people in this manner, the only people who continue to enter the store are the shoplifters! The customers will go elsewhere.

Though our students may not physically go elsewhere, we know all too well that if students get disenfranchised from our classes and schools, they will readily remove themselves mentally and emotionally. Treating everyone—students and adults alike—as if they want to do what is right will make them more likely to do what is right and will help them view us in a much more positive light.

Students—The Most Precious Commodity

It is essential that we also use our students to help rekindle our passion when we need it. Too often we focus on the 5 percent of the students who are the most challenging. However, we are fortunate that the vast majority of our students are a pleasure to work with and to have around. We have to remember what a difference we make.

Every teacher likes to associate with the honor roll students. We can all take a little credit for the valedictorian, and it feels great to do so. However, even without us, the valedictorian may still slide through. Yet, where we may most matter is with the students who are the most needy. For many of these young people we are the highlights of their days and maybe of their lives. It is up to us to determine just how "high" that highlight is. Celebrating all of the young people we work with can be one of the most energizing things we can do for ourselves and one of the most important things we can do for our students. It is important that we make it a point to at least momentarily pause and celebrate the many, many successes that we have. Too often we forget to do so.

One of my college professors told me that back in the old days, when he was a high school teacher, he taught a unit on poetry. When he first started, his goal was to have every sophomore in his class fall in love with the verses that the class was studying. After a while, he realized that this may not have been a realistic expectation. Possibly, not all of the students were going to be swept away in a newfound love for poetry, especially not some of the boys, he thought.

Then one day, at the end of his poetry unit, an overgrown tenth grader, who showed little interest in class in general, much less a love for poetry, came up to him and said, "Before your class, whenever I came across a poem in something I was reading, I always skipped it. Now, because of this class, when I stumble across a poem in a story or article I am looking at, sometimes I actually read it."

We have to hang onto special moments like these and realize that maybe teaching isn't always what we thought it would be. Maybe, sometimes, it is even better.

Those Who Can, Teach

We are probably all familiar with the old and worn-out saying, "Those who can, do, and those who can't, teach." I grew up hearing it in my house on a regular basis. My dad would often repeat that saying. Amazingly, in spite of that, or maybe because of it, I chose to devote my life to education. After many years I realized that my dad was almost right in what he said. Almost.

I believe he just misspoke. Instead, I think what he meant to say was, "Those who can, teach. Those who can't, go into some much less important profession."

We'd like to leave you with one very simple challenge. Approach every day as if you have the most essential job in the world. After all, you do.

REFERENCES

Bissell, B. (1992, July). *The paradoxical leader.* Paper presented at the Missouri Leadership Academy, Columbia, MO.

Burke, K. (1997). *Designing professional portfolios for change.* Arlington Heights, IL: Sky Light Professional Development.

Burr, A. (1993, September). *Being an Effective Principal.* Paper presented at the regional satellite meeting of the Missouri Leadership Academy, Columbia, MO.

Campbell, D., Cignett, P. B., Melenyzer, B., Nettles, D. H., Wyman Jr., R. M., (1997). *How to develop a professional portfolio.* Needham Heights, MA: Allyn & Bacon.

Costa, A. and Garmston, R. (2002). *Cognitive coaching: A foundation for renaissance schools.* Norwood, MA: Christopher-Gordon.

Feigelson, S. (1998). *Energize your meetings with laughter.* Alexandria, VA: Association for Supervision and Curriculum Development.

Fisher, B. (2000). *The teacher book.* Portsmouth, NH: Heinemann.

Goldberg, S. and Pesko, E. (2000). The teacher book club. *Educational Leadership, 57*(8), 39–41.

Gudwin, D. and Salazar-Wallace, M. (2009). *Mentoring and coaching: A lifeline for teachers in a multi-cultural setting.* Thousand Oaks, CA: Corwin.

Harman, A. (2001). A wider role for the National Board. *Educational Leadership, 58*(8), 54–55.

Hartnell-Young, E. and Morriss, M. (1999). *Digital professional portfolios for change.* Arlington Heights, IL: Sky Light Professional Development.

Hopkins Journal (February 26, 1986). Hopkins, MO. Reprinted with permission.

Jenkins, K. (2000). Earning board certification: Making time to grow. *Educational Leadership, 57*(8), 46–48.

Kise, J. and Russel, B. (2010). *Creating a coaching culture for professional learning communities.* Bloomington, IN: Solution Tree.

Livsey, R. and Palmer, P. (2007). *The courage to teach: A guide for reflection and renewal.* San Francisco, CA: Jossey-Bass.

Marzano, R. and Sims, J. (2012). *Coaching classroom instruction (Classroom strategies).* Bloomington, IN: Marzano Research Laboratory.

Richards, J. (Summer, 2011). "Add fun sparkles to your teaching." Kappa Delta Pi *New Teacher Advocate.*

Robbins, P. (1991). *How to plan and implement a peer coaching program.* Reston, VA: ASCD.

Sherin, M. (2000). Viewing teaching on videotape. *Educational Leadership, 57*(8), 36–38.

Whitaker, M. E. (1997). *Principal leadership behaviors in school operations and change implementations in elementary schools in relation to climate.* (Doctoral dissertation). Terre Haute: Indiana State University.